Journey to Inner Light

*A compilation of true stories shared by
truly inspiring people*

Journey to Inner Light

*A compilation of true stories shared by
truly inspiring people*

INNER LIGHT PUBLISHING

Copyright © 2013 Inner Light Publishing.

All rights reserved. No part of this book may be used or reproduced by any means, graphic, electronic, or mechanical, including photocopying, recording, taping or by any information storage retrieval system without the written permission of the publisher except in the case of brief quotations embodied in critical articles and reviews.

All of the stories shared are personal journeys through life and are the responsibility of each author. Inner Light Publishing does not take responsibility for any offense taken by the publishing of these stories and trusts that the author has received relevant permissions to publish them.

Inner Light Publishing books may be ordered through booksellers or by contacting:

Inner Light Publishing
A Division of Adoptamum.com
www.adoptamum.com
innerlightpublishing@gmail.com

Because of the dynamic nature of the Internet, any web addresses or links contained in this book may have changed since publication and may no longer be valid. The views expressed in this work are solely those of the author and do not necessarily reflect the views of the publisher and the publisher hereby disclaims any responsibility for them.

The authors in this book do not dispense medical advice or prescribe the use of any technique as a form of treatment for physical, emotional, or medical problems without the advice of a physician, either directly or indirectly. The intent of the authors is only to offer information of a general nature to help you in your quest for emotional and spiritual well-being. In the event you use any of the information in this book for yourself, which is your constitutional right, the author and the publisher assume no responsibility for your actions.

ISBN: 978-0-9874805-8-3 (sc)
ISBN: 978-0-9874805-9-0 (e)

Printed in Australia

Table of Contents

Prologue   9

A Pearl is a Beautiful Thing   11

A personal story shared by Rhonda Baker about how a challenging journey through life has guided her towards living a love filled life.

Having Faith through Trauma   31

Anonymously shared story about how a road fatality changed the life of a woman filled with spirit.

Accidental Author   35

Inspiring story shared by Andrew Jobling - former St Kilda player now author, writer, mentor and speaker.

Lessons that I learned along the way   59

An insightful journey into the life Mary Lynch, author and columnist, who grew up during a war and has now built a House of Peacefulness.

My Cancer Story   83

Emily Sun shares her journey through cancer and her battle to defy the odds to stay alive for her son.

All for a Reason — 97

A detailed journey by Christie Lyons about her journey to becoming a Soul Sista, writer and childcare manager.

Full Circle — 137

Karen Mc Dermott, author, writer and publisher, shares her journey through the ups and downs of life's lessons that have guided her towards enlightenment.

A Collection of Articles — 165

Articles shared by Andrew Jobling, Mary Lynch, Christie Lyons and Karen Mc Dermott.

Acknowledgements

Inner Light Publishing would like to thank our contributors Rhonda Baker, Andrew Jobling, Mary Lynch, Emily Sun, Christie Lyons, Karen Mc Dermott and our anonymous contributor for sharing their journey in this book. Your stories will touch the hearts of many and hopefully inspire another to aspire towards a more positive outcome to their journey.

We would also like to thank Donna at adoptamum.com; Inner Light Publishing would not exist if it were not for your kind support and belief.

Lastly we would like to convey a message of gratitude to all of our readers.

Prologue

Each of us will endure challenges in our lifetime. Each challenge will be individual to each of us as it visits us under our own unique set of circumstances. Some challenges can be harrowing, some not as bad, but each one is not without reason; through each obstacle there is the potential for growth, and if we open ourselves to the healing that our bodies and minds are equipped to precede such events with, then we have the potential to emerge from such knock downs stronger than we were before.

To know that we have not suffered alone can make a journey more bearable. To know that others have emerged from similar falls can give us hope and comfort. After the darkness there can always be light, after the rain is the potential for a rainbow; have faith that what waits beyond is enlightening. The pain and suffering is not in vain, and we need not be alone.

Shared in this book are a collection of stories that may move you, startle you or comfort you. However the stories connect with you, they are the story of a life that has endured a challenge, but each person has been able to take on board the lessons learned and move forward with their lives in a more positive and aware way.

A Pearl is a Beautiful Thing

A PERSONAL STORY SHARED BY RHONDA BAKER

"A pearl is a beautiful thing that is produced by an injured life. It is the tear [that results] from the injury of the oyster. The treasure of our being in this world is also produced by an injured life. If we had not been wounded, if we had not been injured, then we will not produce the pearl." ~ *Stephan Hoeller*

Today, I look at my life and am glad how it is. I would be lying to you if I said I didn't have moments when I wish it were different—times when I wonder what could have been had I had different experiences. On a not-so-good day, I wonder how much better, richer or successful I might have been had it not been for all the difficulties I have faced. These days are rare though and becoming even rarer. Particularly when compared to the days of rejoicing in having "made it", becoming the person I have, and having achieved more in my life than I ever thought possible. Maturity has helped me realise that this personal achievement has come to me not despite the challenges I have faced but because of them.

These days, I look at the many unhappy faces around me and hear the many complaints of those who have not been though such difficulties. Their lives are not filled with the gratitude, joy, love and many other blessings that I experience on a daily basis. These people are unaware of the many blessings in their lives: the family and friends they have, the money, security and safety they experience on a daily basis. Instead, they often focus on what they don't have and how they see many elements of their lives as problems! The latest financial crises, the rude shop assistant, a bad coffee experience or the software program that isn't good enough. These disappointments fill their lives, and it shows in the unhappiness etched in their faces.

My face is smiling, and I feel a gratitude for the love in my life, for all the joy I experience on a daily basis, and the fact that I *know* I am safe and secure in the world. I am fulfilled by life's simple things: the joy I experience watching my dog run, the sun shining on my face, and the fact that I am loved and can love. I notice that unhappy people don't seem able to experience life as I do. They seem to be blind to the blessings around them and are unable to experience the joy that I know is available to us all.

In searching for my answers, I remember something I read many years ago in a book called *The Secrets of the Rainmaker*. The author Chin-Ning

Chu spoke of the privilege of having a heart broken. I have thought of this many times during my 52 years and can now say I truly understand his meaning. You see, I have had my heart broken many times. The first was when I was three years old and sitting on my bed at home in the dark, hearing yet another terrible argument between my parents. These repeated arguments broke my heart and were absolutely frightening to me. I remember just knowing that I was alone and I was very frightened indeed. So afraid in fact that at this early age, I had perfected my imagination and learnt to bring down soothing coloured lights from the sky above.

The second broken heart came when I was eight years old, with my father creeping into my tiny bed and performing the most distressing and horrifying acts on me. This broken heart was much worse than the first and full of confusion, fear and physical pain. These visits were to be repeated many a time, and my coloured lights were no longer powerful enough to soothe me. Instead, my lights became a person—a white lighted angel, large and loving—and she became my protector, my refuge, and my only safe person. As I grew, I became very good at reading energies and reading people. Despite not being able to actually remove myself from 'bad' people like my father and some others, I knew who they were and could 'remove' myself spiritually, taking refuge in the energy of nature, animals and those few people I felt safe with. There was no one else to save me, and I knew this. My mother had known of the abuse and was powerless to stop it, or perhaps she was so self-consumed that she was distracted by her own world of arguments and hatred, and not mine.

As I grew older, my spirit remained intact with the help of my angel and my ability to connect to nature. But as kind words and bribes were being replaced with physical violence and threats from my father, my teenage-self responded with anger and resistance, making my physical-self suffer all the more. Once again, this abuse was ignored by my mother. Gradually, I came to be extremely independent and in doing so came to reject their model of life. I married when I was 20 to fulfil my dream of having a family of my own and went on to have two of the most beautiful children—just what I had wanted: a girl and a boy. I lived a great life and felt I had finally left the past behind. No need of angels and of coloured lights to remind me of what had been before.

I loved my life and trained as a nurse to fund my husband's medical school training, and I also worked part-time as my children grew. We didn't have much money and my husband was consumed by working and studying, but that didn't seem to matter so much to me. I was living my dream and that was all I wanted: to be a family and to be safe.

My husband was finishing specialist training and needed to work overseas for a time as a result. Reluctantly, I agreed to go. I didn't really want to leave my happy life in Sydney, but we all packed up and went to live in Manchester, UK. This was the start of the unravelling of the life I had worked so hard to build in the previous ten years. I couldn't work part time in the UK as there was massive unemployment at the time. As well, my husband was working very long hours. Consequently, I was alone, with no friends, no family, no money, and limited access to the natural environment I was so used to. Looking back, I now know that I must have been slightly depressed. I had had enough after one year, and I told my husband that I was going home whether he came or not.

So a year before his contract was due to expire, we arrived back in Sydney, much to my relief. I could now get my life back on track and be safe once again, back in the environment I felt so secure in. I had left Manchester three months pregnant and with a virus. We arrived home just before Australia Day, and along with my eldest daughter, who was now seven years old, I was ecstatic. I loved my home, and I loved my life in Australia.

The very first day home, I woke up in pain and with discomfort in my lower abdomen. Within hours, I was bleeding. I was thirteen and a half weeks pregnant. As it was a public holiday, I waited to see the doctor the next day and was told after looking at the scan results that the baby had died. He suggested that it must have been the flu. I was upset but still had my boy and my girl, so I couldn't complain. I was admitted for a small operation and made an easy recovery. We had just moved back into our un-renovated home that was now in worse condition as it had been tenanted out. I was happy though because at least we were home and I could resume my happy life again.

We had been back now about six weeks and everything was going really well. My daughter was in first class, and my son was in preschool two days a week. I was driving him to preschool one Monday, alone as circumstances had it. On that particular day, my back-door neighbour had wanted to take my daughter to school with her own daughter to help me out after my recent miscarriage. Not liking my children driving with other people, I reluctantly agreed, largely due to the carry-on by my daughter at the back fence. So, unusually this morning, it was just my son and me, with him sitting in his booster seat in the back. I had apparently turned left onto a major arterial road and then moved across into the right-hand lane to turn right, waiting there in a stationary position until the oncoming traffic cleared. Suddenly, a tow truck driver travelling at about 80 kph came up behind my still-stationary car, swerving slightly to the left but hitting my car in the process and catapulting us into oncoming traffic, to then be hit at high speed by yet another vehicle. The full impact came on the back passenger door, where my precious son was sitting. My heart was shattered this time.

I sustained a large impact to my head, and my first recollections were of being lifted out of the car and having a man—a policeman, I think—telling me that my son was on his way to the hospital. I remember him telling me how sorry he was but that it was unlikely my son would survive. That is all I remembered of the accident at the time, though a few months later I was told by another school mother that I had been very distressed and was asking where my daughter was. This was to be the first miracle that came from this most horrendous accident. Hearing what happened to the car when my husband viewed it a few days later, it became obvious that the brunt of the impact was on the front left-hand door with the secondary impact being where my son had been sitting. My eldest, being six years old at the time, had started demanding she sit in the front of the car. As the trip to school was really only about three blocks away, she could have easily been sitting at the point of greatest impact. To this day, I feel blessed that there was someone or something looking out for our family and that my daughter's life was left intact.

My beautiful son survived. I have been told that a doctor on his way to work had given him mouth-to-mouth until an ambulance arrived at the scene. He was then taken to our local small hospital just as a very competent Accident and Emergency consultant had arrived at work. He was incubated, stabilized and sent on to the Camperdown Children's Hospital intensive care unit.

The journey of my son's recovery had started, although his life hung in the balance for a further two weeks. Slowly, slowly though, after this very,

very, difficult time, he started towards some sort of improvement. My distress was enormous, and there were so many times I willingly would have taken his place, enduring all the pain and discomfort, the operations and the many distressing results of his brain injury—to endure the things that he had to endure over many, many years. But of course, I was unable to do this.

The next few years were a blur. A few days after my son was admitted to hospital, I went to a previously made doctor's appointment. I was in a daze and do not remember much of what was happening to me at the time, except that he told me I was pregnant. The doctor offered me a termination. I noted this information and then went back to the hospital, told my husband, and continued on with my son's care.

Much to my surprise, my second daughter was born seven months later. I now realise that I had been in a state of shock and denial for many, many months. My son's therapy was intensive, time-consuming and occupied all my available thought processes at the time. Brain injury is a multi-dimensional injury, and the rehabilitation from it is also multi-faceted. His treatment involved consultation with a wide variety of doctors, speech and occupational therapy, as well as physiotherapy, with much of this therapy needing to be reproduced at home. Apart from the multiple weekly visits to the hospital, there was home therapy, which involved such things as swimming, bike riding and exercise regimes. My life revolved around these visits, these exercises and therapies, and my son who couldn't walk or talk for many months. I was consumed, and it was consuming. The only way forward for me was not to think about what needed to be done but just to get on and do it. The labour pains were my first wake-up call to the fact that I was having another child. It was like a thunderbolt of reality hitting me, and very suddenly indeed. What I do know is that this state of mind had allowed me to cope through an incredibly difficult time and that, had I been fully aware of reality, I may not have been able to cope. I think it's called post traumatic shock, or maybe even denial. All I know is it allowed me to get through.

Whilst I had been in denial about having another child, my husband seemed to be in denial about pretty much everything. He went to work, came home, played with the kids, and did nothing much else. He repeatedly told me our son would be fine, shaking his head at me in disbelief at my on-going anxieties, whilst my son still could not speak properly, was not yet walking and seemed to have no idea how to play. In a way though, my husband's denial made me more and more determined to get my son better. My son became my mission, and I was good at missions.

My "perfect" world and my "perfect" life were on their way out. The events of my son's injury brought me into a fast reality of who my husband really was. Despite the very difficult time I was experiencing, all on my own I might add, my resilience and my great, great strength and connection was again coming to the fore. The fact that I had "blocked" out my past to be able to live such a "normal" life was now becoming a limitation, and I was coming to realise that my "perfect" life now felt "numb". The inadequacies and unhelpful ways of my husband were now very obvious to me; however, as a mother to three small children, one with significant disability, I was powerless to change my circumstances. The universe always delivers; when my youngest was four years old, my husband unexpectedly left me for a mutual friend. I was devastated and found it hard to forgive their mutual deceit and betrayal, though as it turned out I found my life no harder. My husband had checked out a long time ago. This then was the start of my greatest healing journey, and I came to realise that my past life with my husband had simply been a breather for someone like me, who had never enjoyed this type of stability before.

Moving on with three children, and having one with a disability and highly complex needs, wasn't easy though. My real break from the past came with moving to my own home in a different suburb. Leaving my "perfect" and happy life behind was made much easier when my best friend of many years—whilst being superficially supportive of me—had not wanted her son to break ties with his best friend who happened to be the son of our mutual "friend", the same friend who had run off with my husband! It was very difficult leaving a ten-year friendship, especially since I really had no one else close in my life at the time. This friend had been more like the sister I never had, but I knew it was necessary. I certainly wasn't willing to have people in my life any more who didn't understand and support me. Being betrayed by that friend had made me very wary indeed of everyone else.

When I look back now, starting my new life was really a very difficult time. I felt so alone in the world and was once again in a place not unlike my childhood: totally alone and unsupported. The universe always has a way of delivering though, and a few days after I moved into my new home, my neighbours came over with their young baby to introduce themselves. It was a strange meeting. After a few minutes with these new people, stories of the husband's recent "cure" from a brain tumour were relayed. I looked at them both with their newborn baby and just knew at that moment that I would see him die. I didn't know how long or when, I just knew that he wasn't going to live.

Our friendship grew from there, and as they had also been through something traumatic recently, we became very good friends very quickly. My children really loved their little baby, and over the next twelve months, my youngest became very fond of the now little toddler who lived next door. At the time, I remember thinking how funny it is that history repeats itself. As a young child growing up, I also used to love playing with the little girl next door. The age difference between the child next door and me was about the same as this little girl and my daughter—about six years—and I think, like my experience all those years ago, it was also a sort of refuge for my daughter. My neighbour announced to me some time later that they were having another baby. Unfortunately, not long after that, the husband's headaches returned, and his quick downhill slide meant that my friend delivered her second child on her own, while at the same time her husband lay dying in the hospital. Our bond became closer because of this, and we were a great support to each other. Unlike friends I had had before, my new friend was incredibly supportive of me. It felt good after never really having had this type of support before. It also became very important to me during this time as I had recently met the man I knew was going to be my next husband.

It had been five years or so since my son's injury, and he was progressing well. There were still the multiple therapies, doctor's visits, etc., but I had learnt with brain injury that once my son had the information drummed into him over many months, it was starting to stick. Catching public transport to his city school was one of the many things we focused on. In all, it took five years till he had it down pat. So, this was the way life had been for me. Feeling I was ready for a good relationship, I had written my list of the qualities I wanted my husband to have. I wanted much more for myself this time, and I wanted to get it right. Despite finding it extremely difficult to launch myself into a relationship again, I did trust that if I wrote my list I would get the right person, eventually. The first time I saw my husband at an arranged dinner, I knew I was going to marry him. I don't know if it was the clairvoyant's description of him or my own inner knowing, but I just knew. I had had a short relationship with another man after my husband had left and this proved very difficult for me. No doubt due to the betrayal of my first husband but also due to my childhood experiences. The trust I had naively put into my first husband I now knew was for survival reasons, and I was not able to do this again. So whilst knowing that he was Mister Right at one level, my anxieties and my ability to have a relationship were very limited. My childhood trauma was resurfacing, and apart from my neighbour and limited times with this new man, my anxieties were spinning me out of control at times. My next door friend was a blessing to me at this time, and she also said I was to her. I knew that I really needed some help and found a psychologist called Gaye who helped women deal with childhood abuse. I hoped she could help.

Meeting Gaye was a blessing, and I felt at ease with her straight away. She seemed to have empathy for my issues despite never having been through such things. I immediately felt comfortable and started revealing to her memories and emotions that I had never revealed to anyone before. I had tried a few therapists previously, but they had proved to be not very helpful; I now felt so lucky that I was able to find this one. The new relationship, whilst opening the door to unbelievable emotions and past events, also unlocked buried dreams for me, and I was now able to hope for the first time in my life for more than just raising children. I remembered my dream to live in the country and own a farm. A difficult step for me, for many reasons I did not at the time understand. Whilst horrendous visions along with silent excommunication by my family made my reality difficult, Gaye became an incredibly important part of my life. Luckily, with her help my relationship with my new partner survived, but only just. I think if I hadn't had that deep knowing that we were meant to be together, there was no way our relationship would have survived. But it did, and I found this man to be of the most unbelievable support.

Something that kept me sane during this time was focussing on my dream I had of having an organic farm. Amazing as the universe is, my first conversation with my new partner was not just about my dream but also of *his* dream of owning a property. I couldn't believe it. We had known each other less than an hour and we were having this conversation! As we talked, we realised that we both had been hankering for a farm for years and both of our now divorced partners had individually held us back, not wanting to pursue such a vision themselves. So, together with my two youngest children in tow, we moved to the most beautiful farm on the south coast of NSW.

Our 68 acre farm was a pure paradise. On my insistence, our farm was run organically, and we decided to start with cattle and sell organic beef. We had purchased a herd of beautiful red Angus cows from a property a few hours' drive from us. After their arrival, despite earlier committing to not naming them, of course we couldn't help ourselves. My husband is a naming "expert" and soon we had Rodney, Robert, Helga, Hilda, and many more, including personalising a few of their numbers, such as Number 40 and Number 30. Despite the incredibly hard work, we absolutely loved the farm and the animals. My partner had a special connection with the animals, and we both felt an enormous connection to this land itself. By this stage, we had decided to get married and agreed on a very simple affair on our farm. We had the celebrant set herself up in our favourite paddock next to a beautiful gum tree that started as one trunk at the base and a short way up became two. We were to get in our farm truck, the "Groover", and met her and our close family members at the tree at 3:00 pm. At this time many of our cows were in calf, and we were a bit nervous about it all but also excitedly awaiting the first birth on our new farm. Just as we were leaving the house and getting into the "Groover", we noticed that in the paddock just next to the house, Number 40 was birthing our first calf. It was so special for us, amazing really, and we both knew that here was a sign of the synchronicity of our lives: our love for each other and the journey we were on. The birth of this first calf at exactly the time of our marriage was our wedding gift—a very special one indeed. Number 40 became our favourite cow, and exactly one year later to the day, very early in the morning of our first wedding anniversary, she delivered her second healthy calf for us. Truly amazing!

I look back now, no longer living on that amazing farm, and I see this thread of connection to nature and how its healing abilities have been with me throughout my life. From a very early age, I desperately wanted a horse, and my first choice for any outing would always have been to be able to go riding. Fortunately, there were a precious few, few occasions where we were all taken riding at a nearby farm. Though I did get to see horses elsewhere, my father was a terrible gambler and he would often take us to the trots on a Friday night. We three children would be left alone in the stands in the general area, and my father would go alone to the member's area. Routinely we would be handed $10 or $20 each, and my older sister, who from the age of twelve looked nearer twenty, would place bets on our behalf and buy us food as we needed. I wasn't too much interested in the bets, but I would absolutely love watching the magnificent horses with their carriages run around and around the track. The lighting, the smell, and the sound of the horse's hooves hitting the ground were all such a mesmerising and connecting event for me. I learnt to love the trots. Also as a child, I would look out the car window at the farms we passed on the way to my parent's business and absorb the energies of them as we drove by. After my son's accident, I would often take the children to the south coast during the school holidays and retreat to the bush and the beautiful beaches there. I have always found this connection with nature essential for my life. In fact, I believe that my ability to make these strong connections in childhood has truly saved my life.

When I now look back over the many years of my life, 52 in fact, I feel that my thread of connection has grown into a web—a web of life. This web now envelopes me and seems to ground me to myself. More of me is connected now, and this connection brings a powerful sense of peace and contentment. I feel very connected to this source, which I believe is part of everything, and of us all. It is not something that we can find at a department store, or in a career or anything that is manufactured or not of nature. I feel very sad when I see how many people live without this connection in their lives. Most are unaware, and sadly there are many who are stuck, living a loveless, joyless and disconnected life. I now understand what is meant when people say things such as "we are all connected" or "we are of the same source". It is so true. It has simply been forgotten by many. This amazing connection protects and sustains us, brings us peace and joy, and binds us all together on this tough, difficult at times, and most amazing journey here on earth. To remember this is to be able to have love and compassion for every human and creature on earth.

For me, connection is my purpose, my reason for being alive. I travel to Thailand twice a year now and assist children in need. I am no hero, no martyr; I simply desire to connect and help where help is needed. This wonderful connection brings me such joy and fulfilment. I feel so grateful to be able to do this, and grateful that the Thais accept my help and allow me to share a connection to their lives. Life can be difficult. Someone once told me that out of these difficult times you need to look for the pearl, the gleaming strong and beautiful object that is a result of all the oysters' hard work. For me, my oyster's hard work was all the difficulties I have faced, and my life's pearl is my ability to connect. It is through this ability that I find love, gratitude, forgiveness and acceptance, and an increasing sense of peace and contentment. Good things to have and more than any riches, success or fame can buy. So, maybe it's not such a difficult life after all!

About Rhonda Baker

Rhonda has dappled with writing for many years. The root of her writing comes from a place of deep connection that she feels compelled to share with others. Her first public writing was a weekly column for the 'Southern Highlands News' on topics of connection such as joy, happiness, emotions etc. Since, she has completed a Masters in Anthropology which gave her the many skills and insight into what is involved in the writing process.

This discipline and experience combined with her need to write about connection, had Rhonda recently finished her first book about her personal journey in Thailand with orphans and street children. Being compelled to share their stories and what it manifested within Rhonda, she has been writing the Orphan Angel Diaries on Adopt a mum.

This wonderful opportunity has given Rhonda the confidence to publish her first book shortly. Life can have each and every one of us forget about our connection to ourselves and each other. Rhonda is motivated to write to remind herself and everyone else, that despite the illusion of being alone we are all on the same journey here on earth.

Having faith through trauma

SHARED BY AN ANONYMOUS LADY TO BENEFIT
THE JOURNEY OF OTHERS

I didn't know that one Thursday morning in March my life was going to change dramatically.

I had a phone call from a stranger, telling me that my husband has been in an accident; it's ok, and he's ok. I'm with him, and he is conscious. She told me where they were and that she had called an ambulance. I said to her, "I'm on my way." I prayed all the way there asking the Lord to take care of him. I think I got there in record time as I got through early morning traffic easily. I couldn't believe what I saw when I stopped my car at the accident scene. His motorbike was a crumpled mess, with bits of it all over the road. I remember kneeling beside him and crying and feeling shock wash over me. He was trying to comfort me with his words even though he was in lots of pain. He told me that the car had pulled straight out into him .The ambulance came, and they put him on the stretcher but every movement for him was excruciating. I rang his mum and then mine and told them what had happened.

My in-laws lived two hours away, so I told them to come up immediately as we don't know the extent of his injuries, even though he is conscious. They took him for tests and x-rays, while I filled out paperwork. By the time they had finished their process, my family and his parents were there. We got to spend time with him before they took him off for surgery. The doctor told us it was a miracle he was still alive, as the force of the hit from the car had torn his aorta, which is the main valve connecting your heart. I'm sure the Lord kept him alive so we could speak to him, and for his parents to see him again.

I am a spirit-filled Christian, which means I have received the gift of the Holy Ghost, with the evidence of speaking in tongues. Since I have received the spirit, I have seen miracles and experienced many healings and provisions. So when he went in for surgery, I knew the Lord had his hand on things. Many people from my church here in Australia and over the world were praying for him. He got through surgery but was in a coma as his brain had swelling too. So many tubes were coming in and going out of his body. The next day, they woke him from his coma, and he talked to us but things weren't right. He was rushed back to surgery and died that night. This was so hard to understand. Why? Why?

I have never cried so much in my life as I had over those days and many more days to come as I would find out. I was angry with God and couldn't pray to him. I had so much love around me from my family and friends but felt so empty inside. Even our dog was mourning the loss as he wouldn't leave my side and would nudge my hand so I would pat him. After two weeks, I realised I need to pray and talk to God again. I needed his comfort. The thing is…. God never left me; Hebrews 13-5: he promises that he'll never leave us or forsake us. He did give me comfort and strength when I thought I had none. I was getting through one day after another.

It was nearly three months on when another bomb shell hit me again. My girlfriend rang me in tears and wanted to talk with me. She came over with a friend and told me that she was truly sorry, but for 18 months she and my husband had been with each other. She kept talking and said she needed to get this off her chest. I asked her questions, which seemed to fill in a few gaps for me. I also spoke to a work colleague of hers to ask if he had been coming to see her at work. After putting it all together, I knew it to be true. It felt like someone had reached into my chest and pulled the last bit of my broken heart out. How is this possible? He's not even here for me to yell and scream at him. It's strange in a way how all this has happened. Yes, it really does sound like a bad mid-day soap story. My tears started to fall again; even sitting in the bath, I remember sobbing my heart out. I was reading my favourite scripture; the Lord says, "I will never let anything too hard for you to bear, or I will make a way to escape." I took off my wedding rings and took down all the pictures of him, after I yelled at them and put them away. My grief stopped, and from then on, I had no more love or tears I was going to shed for him.

So I bet your wondering how can something good come from all this. Well, the answer for me is to trust God—through good times and also bad times.

The months had passed by and my dearest friend became my husband. The Lord had given me a new heart and a wonderful, kind and loving man to share my life with. I felt I was a different person back then to who I am now; I have never been happier, and I have a blessed life now. Who knows why we have to go through trials in our life. We can't change the past, but we can change the future. There is a scripture, 1 Peter 1-7, that says that the trial of your faith, being more precious than gold that does perish; Though it is tried with fire, be found with praise, honour and glory.

ACCIDENTAL AUTHOR

A PERSONAL JOURNEY SHARED BY
ANDREW JOBLING

Born to play sport!

From as early as I can remember I had a ball, a bat, a racquet or ... my brother in my hands!

I loved kicking the Aussie Rules footy with my dad or my brother, and if I had no-one to kick the footy with, I played on my own, kicking a pair of socks around the house pretending to be a champion. I had a hard time explaining to my mum that part of the process of becoming a champion meant that mishaps would occur, such as broken vases caused by flying socks inside the house! When I was old enough, I was on a team and playing the sport with passion.

Playing cricket in the hallway and entrance hall with my brother didn't last long ... for obvious reasons! Soon we were out in the street playing against our neighbours for the Clonmore St cup. That also came to an abrupt halt after a ball, that one of us hit, went sailing through the window, smashing the glass and landing too close (for comfort) to my sleeping baby sister. When I was old enough, I was on a team and giving it my all. My clearest memory was a sunny Saturday—I had been standing in the field for several hours with no action. Finally a high ball came my way, and I sprinted for about 50m and then dived, full length, to take the catch of the year. Well, that was the plan anyway ... I actually dropped the ball and then got up out of the long grass to find dog sh#@ all over my cricket whites. Hilarious for some, tragedy for others!

My mum hated Sundays for one reason: World Championship Wrestling! My brother and I watched and got fired up by the likes of Hulk Hogan, Jesse 'the body' Ventura and George 'the animal' Steele. As soon as it was over, I was jumping off the couch onto my brother, giving him a *flying body slam*! Then he would get me into a *figure-4 leg-lock*, and needless to say, it would end up with something broken and someone in tears ... most commonly me!

I played tennis regularly but, for some reason, never improved. I was really bad at golf—spending most of my time in the bushes, sand or water looking for my ball! I was quite a fast runner so had some success sprinting, and playing down-ball against the wall at school during lunchtimes was a favourite pastime.

It was all about sport!

At the age of about 11 or 12, I realised that my true passion lay with Australian Rules football, and so that particular sport took up most of my thoughts and spare time ... outside of those things I tried hard but couldn't avoid. I would dream of playing at the highest level. I could see myself running out onto the field in front of thousands of adoring fans and kicking the winning goal. The power of visualising combined with hard work saw me fulfill my dream and play professional football from the age of 17–24 years old.

For all the wrong reasons

This pre-occupation with sport—actually a better word would be obsession with sport—meant that other things were forced way down on the priority list. Little insignificant things like school, study, reading and education! I never gave it much thought because I was going to be a professional footballer, so I didn't need it! I am lucky I grew up and didn't just grow older ... and that I had parents who moved me in the right direction!

I did get through school on the bare minimum of effort, with English being my worst subject by far. In fact, the only reason I passed English in year 12 was because I received some tutoring from my mum's best friend and colleague who was the head of English at the same private school at which she worked in Melbourne. This lovely lady was also on the Year 12 English examination board and gave me a few friendly and well directed pointers! Phew!!

So, I finally scraped through secondary school. Then the next step ... oh no, now I had to think about tertiary education. What was I going to do? I was 17 years old and didn't really care as long as it had something to do with sport! I finally decided on a Physical Education degree … Why? Because it sounded like sport to me!

I loved this course! Well, the first two years anyway, as I got to do the things I loved most—play sport, drink alcohol and chase girls! Sure there was a bit of study involved, but I didn't want to overdo it and burn myself out! I really enjoyed learning about different sports … I even got excited about ballet because I learned how to Assemblé, Changement de pieds and of course Plié. One of my favourite party tricks, which impressed the girls and often got me punched by the boys, was my interpretation of a routine … *Assemblé, Assemblé, Changement*!

I was enjoying my course without really any idea of where it was leading me, and to be honest, at that time of my life, I didn't really care! Then in the third year of this four year course, I got a rude awakening … I was told I had to arrange practice teaching rounds. I didn't understand why, and so I went and asked the question. Well, it seemed and was explained to me that I was doing a four year bachelor of education degree … which was a teaching degree. How about that? I was going to be a teacher … who knew?!

It took me a short while to process this new information. Me, a teacher?! I couldn't quite get my head around it—actually it was quite ironic. Not interested in study, just sport. Not a reader or even really that interested in learning. But here I am heading into a teaching career ... for all the wrong reasons! Well, I soon just decided, with the 'fly-by-the-seat-of-my-pants' attitude I lived by, to just go with it—and that is what I did. I became a teacher!

After I somehow successfully completed my fours year tertiary education, I vowed, at that point, that reading was no longer a necessity in my life, and I would give it up. Except, of course, for the essentials: the sports section of the newspaper and comic books! Sure I was going to be a teacher, but I didn't need to read ... that was for the students!!

As you have probably already guessed, my teaching career didn't last that long! I taught for four years, which was long enough for me to realize that I had found a true passion for helping, educating and inspiring others. The challenge I had with teaching teenagers was that most of them didn't want to be helped, educated or inspired by me. So, most of my time was spent trying to get them to just listen to me! I thought I had better get out quickly before I strangled one of them! (Please note—I would never actually strangle a teenager!)

Time to Change

I left my teaching job with mixed emotions ... joy and happiness! With even more joy and happiness I moved into the next career phase of my life—the fitness industry. I became a gym manager for a short time and then moved into personal training. I loved it! It was pay back! I thought back to all the pain and suffering I had been subjected to as a professional footballer by the heartless fitness trainers and I thought, now is my turn to inflict some pain! I gave my clients pain, and then they paid me; it was like a double bonus!

In all seriousness, the reality was that training hard was all I knew. In my mid-twenties when I started personal training, I had just come out of a seven-year career as a professional footballer. For all of those seven years I had been indoctrinated with the attitude and mentality of 'no-pain-no-gain', 'all-or-nothing' and 'go-hard-or-go-home'. During my professional football career, we climbed cliffs and ran up mountains, we carried logs and tractor tyres, and we ran more 400m sprints than I care to remember. I was in pain for most of those seven years! We were yelled at, abused, told we were weak and instructed to just toughen up! I knew nothing more than to train hard—until I felt like passing out, and there were times when I did!

So as I began my personal training career, this was all I knew about training. I trained my clients like I was used to training myself ... with no mercy! If they could walk out after a training session, I felt like I had let them down. If they vomited, I thought it was their way of saying thank you! So, again I am sure you can imagine I was not having a lot of success as a personal trainer! As much as I was enjoying myself, my clients were getting injured, not getting results, they were cancelling regularly and even not showing up at all. My initial thought was that they were soft, weak and they needed to toughen up. But after some reflection, I realized the problem ... I was an idiot!

Maybe idiot is a strong word—the reality was that I didn't know what I didn't know. I was under the mistaken impression, as a result of my experiences, that the secret to being healthy, lean and happy was exercise. I simply and naively thought that if you trained often enough, long enough and hard enough, you could achieve any result you wanted. In this conclusion, however, I failed to take into account two important considerations; the first was the power of food and good nutrition in this whole process. The second and maybe more critical was the fact that most people don't want to be professional athletes! They just want to be fitter, leaner and healthier.

To change my thinking from a hard core, all-or-nothing approach to one which promoted balance and enjoyment was a difficult shift for me. I remember clearly, after I decided to place more importance on nutrition, throwing myself into some intense learning about the power of food. I actually read some books—even though I vowed that I would never read again! I researched, I learned, I experimented and I developed an eating plan for myself that many people would call extreme ... just like my training regime.

I decided if I was going to do it I would do it properly. So I gave up sugar, chocolate, desserts, fat foods and I ate lean, natural, fruits, vegetables and proteins. I became one of those really painful people—you know the ones you go out with? I ordered salad with the dressing on the side, no sauces on my food, and I tried to change every meal on the menu to suit my extreme eating standards ... boy was it stressful! Then if that wasn't stupid enough, I tried to make my clients eat the same way!! Yep ... dumb!! They still kept cancelling, but now they would also just conveniently forget their food diaries to avoid the wrath of their psycho trainer (me) who would berate them for eating the most miniscule amount of chocolate!

I am obviously a slow learner, but eventually I did get it. I finally learned the concept of balance, moderation and enjoyment, and I developed a simple formula that was working for myself and my clients. I would talk about this concept with people, many of whom would ask if there were any good books on the subject. I thought about it and finally came to the conclusion that there were none ... none that were user friendly for most people. Of the books I read, they all suggested, promoted or discussed methods that required some kind of complicated or extreme approach, such as: don't eat carbs after 3 pm, don't combine protein & carbs, fruit only before midday, no carbs at all, count calories, weigh this & measure that, be careful of your blood type, etc.

An Unreasonable and Illogical Decision

Now I am not saying these books are wrong or bad; what I am saying is that, for most people, they are too hard to implement & maintain, and most people will never stick at them long enough to get results. They weren't lifestyle-friendly books. So at this point in my life when I was working seven days per week in my own personal training business and my own café, I made the most illogical decision I have ever made ... I decided I was going to write a book!!

When I cast my mind back to that decision at that time, I am incredibly grateful that I didn't think about it too much. Why? Because it was a totally unreasonable decision for me to make, and if I had thought about for even a second, there is no doubt I would have talked myself out of it. I was already working 12–15 hour days, seven days per week. I was a footballer and a personal trainer who vowed I would not read any more books other than comics or the sport section of the newspaper. I only just passed English in year 12. Who possibly would or could have connected Andrew Jobling with author; it does not compute!

So it was in my ignorance and naivety, without too much thought and without asking anyone else what they thought about the idea, I just started writing. I had no idea what I was doing or really how I was going to get it done. All I knew was that this book would be written and that it would make a difference in the lives of others. I have learned that this is one of those principles of life and success: when you know what you want, why you want it and if you want it badly enough then you will always work out how to get it done.

My first major obstacle was my belief in my ability to be an author. But I reasoned that if I can speak and I can communicate verbally with clarity, then I can write so that people can understand. Secondly, the thought of what it would take to write a whole book was pretty daunting. But then I asked myself, what is a book? It is just a group of words strung into a sentence, a whole heap of sentences that form paragraph, lots of paragraphs to make up a chapter and a handful of chapters that create a book! Simple! So really, a book is written just **one word at a time** ... I can do that! The last hurdle I could see was finding the time to write, but I just found small regular pockets of time. An hour here, 20 minutes there and over time ... guess what? One word and one day at a time I had written a 50,000 word manuscript ... okay, now what?!

Simple, find a publisher who loves my manuscript! I have to admit here that I don't have the inspiring story of the author who had to overcome dozens and dozens of rejected submissions from publishers. I can't say that I was living in the streets and eating scraps out of garbage cans with my unpublished manuscript as my only hope for survival. I wish I could tell you the great story of pain, suffering and my overcoming insurmountable odds to get my book published! I hate to say that my first two books were actually quite easily published!!

It turns out that there are publishers in my family! So getting my manuscript looked at was easy. Having them accept the manuscript, even though they were family, was not quite as easy, as it still had to be a commercially viable proposition. So when they said they would publish it, I knew it had to be good enough for them to think it would be profitable! I was excited! Then the publishers even asked me to write another book for them ... one to go into a series of wellness books they produced. Of course I said yes!

So two years after I had unreasonably and illogically decided to become a published author, with really no qualifications, no writing skills and no idea how it could or would happen ... it actually happened! Proud, excited and to be honest a bit stunned, I held, in my hands, my first two published books: ***Eat Chocolate, Drink Alcohol and be Lean & Healthy*** (***Eat Choc*** for short) and ***Simply Strength***! Both, by the way, became best-sellers!

There is no doubt about it ... I am an accidental best-selling author!

The Passion Begins

I had accidently discovered the most burning passion I had or have ever found (with the exception of my beautiful wife Laura). Writing was it

... who could have possibly predicted? Certainly not I! I really had no idea if my books would sell, I had no idea if anyone would read them, and if they did I had no idea what they would say. Then not long after the release of **Eat Choc,** I was stunned to receive this email from someone I had never met:

> "Andrew, I googled your name wondering if you have written another book and discovered your email address. Your book has had a profound effect on my life. My 14 year old son bought the book for me for Christmas as he was concerned about my weight. Ironically he bought it from the Margaret River Chocolate Factory while we were on holiday. It has changed my life - I stopped weighing myself after I had lost 25 kgs from 110kgs and use my belt and watch band to gauge my progress. My whole family has embraced GI and your holistic approach towards life - exercise, nutrition etc. I push your book to everyone who asks how I did it.
>
> Thank you."

Who knew I could have such a profound impact on another person's life? Someone I didn't even know! It was incredibly mind blowing but also unbelievably empowering ... I was hooked. That was the start of my new obsession! As a result of writing my books I was now more able to get speaking arrangements at different places, and I had really found my place in life. I was doing what I had always done—that is, helping people to be fitter, leaner, happier & healthier—but now I could impact more people than just working one-on-one with them. I was excited!

My only small obstacle was time! I was working 12–15 hour days in a business that I couldn't remove myself from. Whilst I was there I couldn't do the writing and speaking I wanted to do. So after 15 years of personal training I knew if I didn't find a way to get myself out then I would start to resent it. So the question was: how do I create time without losing my income so I can focus on this new and incredibly burning passion of mine?

Through this process I had actually decided that now as I am an author, I should probably start reading myself! So, I did and for that I am incredible grateful. Whilst reading a couple of personal development books, I discovered the solution to my time and money issue. The first, **Rich Dad, Poor Dad** by Robert Kiyosaki explained to me the difference between passive and active income and why, if I wanted time and money, I needed to create a passive-style income. The second, I can't remember the name of it, talked about the idea of giving up what you want in the short term to get it back in abundance for the long term.

So, I did. I took the advice of both authors, and for the next 12 months I invested any time outside of my busy life to creating a passive income. This enabled me to go from working 80–90 hours per week to 30 hours a week without losing any income!

It really worked; for just 12 months I gave up 5–10 hours per week that I would rather have spent writing to get back 50 hours per week that I could use any way I wanted! It was amazing and a dream come true because now I could focus on my passion: writing, speaking and helping others.

The Next Book—Heart-breaking

Through much of my adult life, as I was struggling to find myself, my passion and my direction, I had an inspiring person beside me and behind me keeping me going when I felt like giving up. It was my mum, Sue. When I was in my mid-twenties and in my teaching years, she was diagnosed with breast cancer which quickly spread to her liver. The doctors' prognosis was not optimistic, and they gave her only a few more years to live ... but they didn't know my mum!

She didn't listen to what the doctors said—she had a life to live, places to go and people to love. Her next 15 years were the source of great overcoming, persistence, strength, love, joy and happiness. They were years that taught me the power of a decision and the strength of an attitude independent of even the most challenging circumstances. My mum is my hero, and she inspired me then, as her memory continues to inspire me today.

So, in September 2004 I was on a holiday on the Gold Coast with my mum and dad and my partner, at that time. At this point my mum had been battling her breast and liver cancer for 15 years, and during those years, as I mentioned, she had absolutely inspired me with her vision, her courage, her determination and her incredible attitude and will to live a great life no matter the circumstances. It was then I got the idea for my next book … I made a decision during that week away that I was going to write it about my mum; I would share her story and the lessons to inspire the world.

We had a great week as a family, and I particularly wanted to spend some special time with mum to talk to her about her life and journey with the disease. So, on one of the days I told her that I was planning to write a book about her life to highlight some valuable lessons that could benefit others. Her response was: *"Why would anyone be interested in my story?"* She had such humility and quiet determination about her which I struggle to find the words to describe. For hours we talked, we laughed, we cried, I listened and I wrote, and at the end I was even more proud of and inspired by mum and totally determined that this book would be written.

Well, we all have great intentions and then along comes life to bite us in the butt! It was only a couple of months after this trip to QLD that, due to an extreme course of radiotherapy, my mum's condition rapidly deteriorated. She went from being this active, mobile and vibrant women to being so incapacitated that even just sitting up in bed was a huge challenge.

The one thing, however, that didn't change was her 'never give in' attitude and the beautiful smile with freshly applied lipstick that was always on her face! That is the last memory I have of my mum as she slipped into her final peaceful state on December 3, 2004.

I had 15 years to deal with the fact that my mum had cancer and that there was a chance that she may die before her time—but did I? Not for one second! My head was buried far too deeply in the sand just hoping it would all go away, so when it happened I was devastated. The next 12 months was an absolute write off! The only thing that happened, within that period of time, to distract my grief for my mum was the break down of my long-term relationship. When it rains!!

Over the next couple of years it was really all about trying to make some sense of the things that had happened. It was a confusing time, and so any thought of a book was at the farthest reaches of my mind. But, as they say, 'time heals all', as does perspective and a desire to find the good in all situations. I started to write spasmodiacally over the next couple of years and got about half way into the manuscript. The decision finally came in May 2008, whilst I was on my honeymoon with my beautiful wife Laura, that it was time to finish what I had started. I got back to work, this time with a determined focus to finish the manuscript.

Once it was finished I was excited! I thought it would be a simple job to get it to my publishers and then let them do the rest. What I wasn't expecting was that they <u>didn't</u> want it!! What do I do now? After the initial shock I started making calls and sending manuscripts to about 20 publishers, and then I waited. One by one they all rejected the manuscript! I started to doubt myself and wondered whether this was ever going to happen. Then I thought about my mum—her attitude, her resilience, her determination—and needless to say, I kept going!

Next approach …! I started to contact literary agents the same way I did publishers and got a pretty similar result. Until one day, I got a call! One literary agent, whom I will be eternally grateful to, said she would take my manuscript and find me a publisher, and she did. So in July 2009 ***Exisle Publishing*** accepted my manuscript—nearly five years after I began!

I thought it would be easy from here. The editor read the manuscript thoroughly and sent me an email. She started the email with: *"I've put some very rough ideas down for how I think the manuscript and general approach needs to be reworked."* Then she finished the same email with: *"Hopefully I haven't shocked you into depression!"* I wasn't depressed; however, I was overwhelmed! But I got to work to rewrite and improve a vast majority of the book. After much to and fro'ing and some very confronting changes in thinking and approach to the manuscript, it was finally finished. On October 29, 2010 I got an email from the editor saying, *"Just to let you know that your book is now at the printer"!!!* On Monday January 10, 2011, some six and half years after starting, I received my first, finished hardcover copy of ***Dance Until it Rains***!

This is one of the best feelings I have ever had in my life. Writing this book in particular was the most challenging but the most rewarding and, to be honest, the most healing thing I have done to date. Losing my mum was heartbreaking, and for a long time I actually couldn't see the light at the end of the tunnel. The process of writing her story gave me a new perspective about her life and death. I could finally see the light—I could finally see the purpose.

Through my mum's life I could now see her purpose was to bring a flash of light and hope to this planet and to the people she impacted. Through her death I can now see her purpose, with me, is to share the lessons that can help many people live a great life and have a similar impact on others. When I really got this, I could think about my mum not with sadness but with joy and gratitude. She is not gone, she is with me every day, and I believe that together we are changing the world.

All it takes is … One Word at a Time!

I am forever impacted and inspired by the power of the written word. I now know—through the process of writing about my mum—that everybody has a story which needs to be shared and will inspire others. I realised that if I can be an author then anybody can be an author—and I mean <u>anybody</u> and <u>everybody</u>!

I decided that I was going share this accidental, new found passion with others to encourage and help them to experience the same joy that I now experience. So I developed a workshop called ***One Word at a Time*** specifically designed to help anyone, no matter their background, age, education, skill level or self-belief to write and publish and sell their own book. My reasoning was simple: if I can do it, anyone can do it. Everyone has a book in them that needs to be written and shared.

The reality is that all it takes to write a book is just one word at a time! The key factor for me has never been ability, technique, literary knowledge or most other things that people believe it takes to be an author; I never had any of those attributes. For me it was simple: start writing <u>one word at a time</u> and keep going until it is finished—that is it. The simple secret of success: **finish what you start!**

With this in mind my workshop was created; first, a face-to-face workshop, and then in late 2011 it went online—. Since that time and until now (February 2013) over 4000 people all around the world are at some stage of the 10-module workshop, and I am proud to say that, so far, ten people as a result of my workshop have written and published their very own book. These are people who, like me, had no idea they could! They didn't know how to, they just knew why they wanted to. As a result, they are now changing lives of people they don't even know! Can you see why this is such an incredible passion for me?

I still laugh today when I think of what has had to happen in my life to go from where I was to being a passionate writer and author. The series of events that have, seemingly by accident, led me to this point where I can now influence and help many thousands of people to do something they had no idea they wanted to do or even could do is surreal. Life is an amazing and exciting place of possibility and surprise!

The moral to my story is that there really are <u>no accidents</u> in life! We create our destiny by dreaming bigger than most people would think reasonable, by believing in ourselves more than most people would think sensible, by making decisions that most people would think illogical and continuing to act way beyond the point that most people would have given up.

It is your life, live it by choice and enjoy the seemingly accidental pleasures that come to you in abundance! Andrew Jobling, February 2013

About Andrew Jobling

Andrew Jobling played senior AFL football for the St Kilda Football Club — But don't hold that against him! He has over 25 years experience in educating, speaking, business development, leadership, training elite athletes and health & wellbeing.

As a personal trainer he yelled at lots of people for many years before he discovered the secret to helping them achieve long term success with their health, mind and body.

As a business owner he worked ridiculous hours with many different people before he discovered some powerful insights!

He learned some incredibly profound and life changing lessons from his courageous and inspiring mother as he observed her 15 year cancer journey which ultimately took her life. Andrew passionately narrates and describes this journey and these lessons in his new book *'Dance Until It Rains'*.

ACCIDENTAL AUTHOR ~ ANDREW JOBLING

Andrew is the author of the bestselling *'Eat Chocolate, Drink Alcohol and be Lean & Healthy'* & *'Simply Strength'* and his third book *'Dance Until It Rains'* has just been released.

He is a dynamic, entertaining and inspirational speaker who spends his time sharing the secrets that have changed countless lives.

Andrew assists aspiring writers through his 'One Word at a Time' online workshop and is offering a VIP service for Inner Light Publishing readers
www.andrewjobling.com.au/one-word-at-a-time/one-word-at-time-vip

VIP redemption code: INNERLIGHT

Supporting the OLIVIA NEWTON JOHN CANCER & WELLNESS CENTRE through his work

ANDREWJOBLING.COM.AU

Lessons that I learned along the way

A PERSONAL STORY SHARED BY MARY LYNCH

I believe your life journey starts the day you are conceived, and then you are born into your lessons for this lifetime—lessons, I believe, that your soul chooses for your spiritual growth.

I was born in June 1959 into a region in Ireland that had been hovering on the brink of political violence for a long time but was fairly peaceful when I arrived as the sixth child. Six more were to be born after me. By the time my youngest sister had arrived ten years later, Northern Ireland was locked in crisis. Catholics had started to march for equal civil rights, and Protestants fought back to maintain the status quo. The British Army were originally brought in to defend the Catholic population against this backlash, but within a short period of time, they were engaged in the conflict and had begun to inflict violence on the Catholic and Nationalist community.

I became a teenager in 1972, a year that started with the British Army shooting dead 14 Catholics on the streets of Derry (seven of them teenagers) as they marched to protest against the state policy of internment (indefinite imprisonment without trial), which was used nearly exclusively against the Catholic population.

By the end of the year, there were 495 people dead (three of them were neighbours and friends), and it was to be the worst year of the troubles in terms of deaths. It was a year that changed my life.

Twenty nine years later—the night before my book went to final edit—the British Prime Minister, David Cameron, apologized to the people of Derry for what happened on Bloody Sunday. I wrote a poem that night which became part of the book. I named it after the year.

1972.
Adolescence beckoned with great expectations,
Innocence of youth, expectations of the innocent
365 days, 495 deaths later, it ended,
With the loss of that innocence and the death of those expectations.

By the end of that year, I had crossed a line that no one should ever have to cross—I had decided I would kill if necessary to save my family from the lethal and heavily armed British security forces that stalked our farming neighbourhood in the dead of night.

From that time, I slept terrified with one eye open waiting for them to come, planning to use my father's shotgun to save us. A year later, I woke with a gun at my head, a British soldier at the end of it ordering me out of my bed. That night we all stood at gunpoint in our bare feet in the kitchen, and for the next few hours, our house and whole life was ripped apart. As I looked across the fields to our neighbours and saw the light go on in their cowshed, I believed that they would never see us alive again

That night the war that was outside our house came into our home; a home that was never to be the same again. My father, the man who was our protector, could not protect us from this. Years later, I wrote a poem about that night.

My Mother.
She stood in her own kitchen.
He stood in front of her in a foreign land.
She had ten children behind her.
He had an army and two governments.
"Where is your son," he said?
"I don't know," she replied.
"You don't know where your fucking son is," he spat.
"No," she answered.... "Does your mother know where you are?"

They came often after that first time, and the soldiers usually left with one of my seven brothers in tow. That first night, I built a wall around myself to protect me—a wall that took a few hours to build but over thirty years before I could even begin to dismantle it.

Our home became part of a war zone as some of my brothers, like many local men, got involved in the IRA (Irish Republican Army). I continued in school, working hard to survive this change, and I left at sixteen wanting to become a nurse; however, it was not to be, so I went to college to train as a hotel receptionist.

In 1977, at the age of eighteen I was working in a local hotel when it was bombed. I was the only person who saw the man who planted the bomb (he booked in and then left the device in the bedroom), and I was questioned by the police. When they discovered my family's association with the IRA, they came back the next day and took me. For the next 24 hours I was held illegally and tortured by them. Again, I did not believe I would survive. In fact, I prayed that I would die; I prayed that the gun they threatened me with would give me freedom from this nightmare. The freedom I saw only in my death as they played Russian roulette with my head. Worse were the things they said they would do to me, the worst kind of sexual vilification and abuse that I can never forget.

I was traumatized and in shock when I was thrown out of an army Saracen on a dark winter's night. In the hours that followed, a voice told me not to tell a soul what they did to me. I knew I would be unable to live with the consequences if I had. The police interrogators had told me that they would send a gang of Loyalist murderers, trained by the Shankill butchers (a group of psychopaths that tortured Catholics to death and then dismembered the bodies) to kill all my family, starting with my mother, if I ever told.

I also realized that if I told anyone, there would be reprisals by the IRA which would have continued with retaliation from the security forces against our community: a vicious cycle.

Shortly after this incident, I left the North of Ireland, never to return there to live. I went first to Dublin, from there to Germany and then to New York. In 1983, I got married in the US to a man from the West of Ireland and returned to live close to where he was born after six years in exile. There I hoped to live in peace whilst being able to visit my family in the North. Two days later, my brother was shot by the SAS on a shoot-to-kill policy. He survived, but his comrade was shot at point blank range as he lay on the ground. Again I was silenced, afraid to speak of my past. It triggered buried trauma. I went on autopilot and grimly continued with my life, blocking the trauma by becoming a workaholic.

A year later, my first child was born in the North. Looking back, I think I chose the hospital because I wanted to make peace with the town in which I had been so traumatized. If peace and healing were indeed my motive, this was not to be.

Before Roisín was born, a bomb was planted in the town. Fourteen people were killed and their bodies lay in the morgue of the hospital when she was delivered. The horror of this awful thing triggered my memories again, forcing me to work harder and harder to keep the memories at bay.

I worked fourteen-hour days as I bought, renovated, and rented properties. I also provided accommodation for psychiatric patients for the local health board, while running a home for my family.

My son Jarlath was born two years later in 1990. By 1993, I was surviving on work and meditation, barely able to eat. I was like a runaway train that did not know how to stop. I later realized that this happens in life until your own body eventually stops you. Mine finally did. I ended up in the local doctor's office, exhausted and depressed.

"Mary", he said, "This is the best thing that ever happened to you."

I could not believe what he was saying. How could he say this? I was on the edge. In time I realized how right he was. My body had forced me to take a long hard look at myself, but first I had to go on antidepressants.

Drugs, I now realize, are a short-term solution to a long-term problem. The first medication didn't work; in fact it made me much worse. The second prescription worked, but even with taking it, I was still suffering.

In 1994, there was a ceasefire in the North, and for the first time ever I felt that my family were safe. I started to reduce the medication until I was free from prescription drugs. I then started the journey back to myself. A long lonesome journey, as I knew no one who could understand why I was suffering. I had buried it so deep, even I had forgotten.

Flashbacks rained in on me like a hail of bullets. I had no choice but to start looking for help. A psychotherapist told me I was suffering from Post-Traumatic Stress. No words could describe the relief of knowing what was wrong with me.

At this point, I had been meditating and visualizing for over fifteen years, so I started to encourage these memories to surface in my meditations. I created a room in my mind where I would take each memory and deal with the trauma it had left in my body. I would watch as each wound was healed. I knew it would take a long time but understood that every journey starts with the first step and knew that these steps were in the right direction. I knew I had to allow the pain that had been imprisoned in my body to express itself before I could let it go. I started to practice Tai Chi, which gave me physical, mental and emotional strength.

Emotionally I was still a traumatized teenager. I would react to situations like a teenager. I had been forced to grow up overnight but my emotional state did not, could not. It had frozen in shock.

My marriage was in a shambles. My husband couldn't understand what had happened to the capable woman he married. He wanted me to stay on drugs. It was my marriage or my sanity. I chose my sanity. We split up.

He moved to a house which we owned next door, giving our children access to both of us. That night he left, I explained to them what and why I was suffering. This opening up to them was something he would never have allowed. I told them that I would be ok but I had to face things from my past that needed to be dealt with. If they were to come into a room and find me crying, it was ok. It was all part of a natural healing process.

I tried to keep this process to meditations or nights when they were fast asleep, but it was not always possible. Sometimes they would find me rolled in a ball, frightened and afraid.

Life went on, and in time I learned to trust my Tai Chi teacher. I needed to tell someone my story, and I chose him. He had offered when he first saw me in distress; I laughed at the idea that I would ever tell him anything. He was everything I despised; he was English and looked like a British soldier.

The more I told him, the more surfaced. I realized very quickly that to tell your story you needed to open up the wound. Yet, in standard therapy, fifty minutes after you opened up to your therapist you were supposed to close down again and go back to everyday life until the next scheduled therapy session. I found this impossible. It was impossible to blank it until I was free to open up again. Unable to tell my friends and family what was happening to me, I bought a little cottage in the mountains and went there to allow the normal healing process to continue. I decided if I ever got better I would open up such a place for others on the same journey as myself—a safe place where someone could go, where others would understand this process and support them should they require it.

The long process of facing my pain and my buried memories continued as my children went through their teenage years, triggering so many memories of myself at that age. I found myself feeling emotions that I had never felt before, feelings that had been stunted by the shock I had suffered—anger, jealousy, infatuation, love. It was a very difficult but rewarding time as I matured into adulthood at the same time as my children.

During this time, I bought a site beside my cottage in the mountains. I decided to use this site to build the house where mental and emotional healing could take place for people like me. It would be a safe and welcoming house where people going through trauma could come to allow the natural healing process to occur. I was frightened of starting another project, frightened that it would push me over the edge again, but something told me to just do it.

This project I started with my brothers (all builders) when the country was experiencing a boom. When the bubble burst, I was left with a house half finished, two children at university and no money.

"What happens next?" I wondered. But now, instead of reacting adversely to things that happened, I was very conscious of the journey I was on. It was a journey that had directed me to my true self, my own power to heal and with the intention of helping others on this journey back to themselves, realizing their potential to heal themselves.

It was Christmas 2008; I put everything to the back of my mind as I celebrated the holidays with my family. On New Year's Day, I drove up North to meet my parents and siblings. As I crossed the border, the feeling that I was home filled every cell of my body. The peace and love that flowed through me was the most wonderful feeling I have ever had. It was because in my heart I had found a peace that I knew would travel with me wherever I was to journey for the rest of my time on this earth—a peace that I had been seeking for nearly forty years, a peace that no land, nobody or nothing could give me, a peace that I had finally found in myself.

Two days later, I returned to the west. Next morning as the children slept soundly in their beds,

I headed to the kitchen to tidy up the mess from the night before. I tuned in to the national radio station to drown my thoughts of what was to come next, to listen to a presenter that I had spoken to on air about post-traumatic stress. He was not on that morning. As I reached to turn off the radio the woman presenter said, "If you have ever thought of writing a book stay tuned. We have one of Ireland's best writers to tell you how."

I continued to move my hand to the switch when a voice in me said, "You can write a book!" This voice had been guiding me for years now and even though I laughed out loud I didn't switch it off. I smiled at the idea as I continued cleaning the kitchen.

When the presenter came back on air after ads, I picked up my pen to write down the magic formula. I wrote 2,000 words a chapter, 100,000 words for a book. I smiled again as I reminded myself that I had failed my English twice. My hand reached the switch for the second time as the author said, "It took me six weeks to write the first 2,000 words."

I hesitated for a moment. That may be possible I thought. I turned off the radio and turned on the computer. Two hours later I had 2,000 words, and I knew I was going to write a book. I did. It took me two weeks to finish the story of my life and of my struggle to freedom.

I convinced myself that I wrote it for my children, but I knew it was going to be published. These things are very obvious when you open your eyes. Mine were now wide open, and I was scared. I had told my story just as it happened. No holds barred. I now had to face the fear of letting it go. I had wanted to hide it, still frightened of reactions from myself and from others.

Eighteen months later, it was launched in the town that I had lived in for over twenty-five years. A place where everyone thought they knew me but no one did. The whole town turned out, and I talked about it in public for the first time in my life—for all of three minutes. Within a week, I was doing half an hour on radio stations and on TV without a problem.

The night it was launched, a friend brought an acquaintance of his with him, a man that he had insisted that I meet. I shook his hand, and no more was said. Two days later, he emailed me asking me to a meeting of a group called Renew. I hesitated as I had never dealt with groups, always worked alone, but my inner voice told me to go. I didn't hesitate.

When it came to my turn to introduce myself to the group I said, "My name is Mary Lynch. I have just had a book published about my journey, where I not only survived but have thrived. I have a house in the mountains that I want to open to support others with their journey."

One of the group immediately responded, "We too want to open houses to support people on their journey. Renew is a group of people who understand that the experience of psycho-spiritual distress is a healing and renewal process and not an illness but a natural part of life."

I knew then why I had come, that I was in the right place and I had found the right people. But I was not ready to move to the mountains, as my children still needed me at home.

A few days later, my sister called to ask if I would mind if she contacted the local paper in the place where I was reared, to ask them if they would review my book.

"Go ahead", I replied, but I was frightened. This was where my torturers still lived. The paper was read mainly by the other side of Northern Ireland's religious divide. I was surprised when the editor said he would be delighted to. When I read his review, I was astonished by such compassion and understanding from a man from the other tradition.

One of the things he said in his review was that the book had been written without anger. The anger had been written on hundreds of pages of scribbled bitterness in my bed on those long dark nights of the soul, whilst my children lay sleeping in the next rooms. All these pages were burned a week before New Year's Day 2009. The day I felt peace saturate every cell of my body. A week before I started the book!

While my own healing was taking place, political reconciliation and empowerment was finally healing the wounds in the society of my birth. A peace agreement had been reached, and for the first time, Catholics were encouraged to take part in government. One of my sisters became a county councillor. My brother, who had been shot, then jailed for twenty five years for being a member of an illegal organization, was now in politics and was campaigning for election to Stormont, where he now represents his community.

I had never stopped writing from Jan 2009 and had a second book written within months. I filed it, and then started to write other people's stories as they were told to me. They were ordinary people with extraordinary stories. I had found a passion; I loved writing.

A few months later, I woke and my wee voice told me to call the editor who had written the review and ask him if he would be interested in publishing the stories I had written. I never questioned the voice. I just called his number. He took my call immediately.

"What can I do for you Mary?" He asked.

"I've written a lot of true short stories of other people's lives, and I wondered if you would be interested in publishing them?"

"I would", he replied.

"Don't you want to read some of them?" I asked, laughing.

"Of course I do", he replied, "but I am interested. Did you see how I have just changed the format of the paper?"

I had not the heart to tell him that I never bought nor read his paper in my life. That it would not have been allowed to darken the door of our Catholic home as we were growing up. Even though my family were now buying it and had been for a few years—things were changing.

"I will edit a few and send them to you", I said, instead.

Then I panicked as I didn't know how to edit and knew that I would have to send in a finished product every week. I called my publisher. She said, "I will teach you how, but in the meantime get someone else to help."

I called the editor the next morning.

"I don't know how to edit yet, and I don't want to waste your time or mine. Can I read you a story?"

"Yes", he replied.

I read, and then held my breath.

"That is brilliant, Mary," he said, "It doesn't need to be edited. It is perfect the way it is."

And so, I began to write each week and have been ever since. Real stories of people's lives and the lessons they've learned—helping others to understand that they are not alone.

During this time, people started to come to see me, people who had read my book and columns and wanted support to move on. I helped them with the support of the group Renew.

The first real cry for help was from man, who emailed me saying, "Hi Mary, my name is Gerry. I am from Belfast. I have just finished your book, and for the first time in thirty five years, I see a light. Please can I come to see you?"

I was shocked that someone from that war-torn city could understand my story and wanted my support. For too long I had believed that I should not tell my story because there were people worse off. I now understood that by telling my story I helped others tell theirs.

I emailed back giving him my home number and saying, "Please feel free to call me."

I went for a walk and on my return found that he had called three times. One of the messages said, "I filled my car with petrol today. Can I come tomorrow?"

I was still living in the family home as my children finished their third level education. He asked me to book him into a local hotel as he needed to rest after the long journey. He arrived at the appointed time, six on the dot. We sat in front of the fire until 11, only rising to make tea.

He came back the following morning, and we went for a walk and talked some more, agreeing to meet again.

"You cannot be letting strangers into your house, Mary," my friend had advised.

"He is not a stranger," I replied, "He is someone on the same journey as me."

He returned a few times, and then I invited him to the cottage to stay with me and a friend. When he was leaving he said, "You need a lot of work done here before you can take people to stay. I am a carpenter. I will do it for you."

"Thanks Gerry," I replied, "But I have no money. I can't afford to pay you."

"I want no payment," he replied, "Only your ear, your lovely meals and your friendship."

In the next few weeks, I watched my cottage being transformed. He was also there to help when others in distress arrived. The house was up and running. When my son finished college, I moved bag and baggage.

I was very cautious in what I was doing as no one else in the country was doing anything like it. "What if someone comes in complete distress?" I asked my Renew friends one night. "I am not equipped to do this alone. Will I have the support?"

Only one of them was able to offer it. "Ok," I replied, "Then we can't do it." Not long after that, one such case arose. I told her, "Get on a train and come to me." I didn't care if there was no one to help. I knew the lord would provide.

She arrived on a wet wintry evening. She was lost and lonely. I met her and spent most of the night sitting with her as her distress poured out. She wept and cried out in anger.

The next day, two people from Renew arrived, and before the week was out others were coming from all over the country to support her. She stayed for six weeks. Many others have come since and found a safe haven where they can rest from their struggle or confront their demons in the company of sympathetic and caring friends—peer to peer support.

Meanwhile in the grip of recession, I tried to sell some property, but nothing was moving. I was broke, and the bank was putting pressure on me.

"I'll help you sort out the house in Belfast," Gerry told me. "Drop the price and get rid of it."

I moved in with him and his girlfriend for a week, and we worked on it together. He had me up at 5:30 every morning, and we worked twelve hour days. A week later, it looked so good I wanted to stay there myself.

Two days later it sold.

This left me with enough money to get the banks off my back for a while. It also left me with enough money to finish the new house I had started five years earlier and pay off all my debts to my family, who had supported me whilst I struggled financially.

For the next three months, my brother came every Monday morning and went home on a Friday evening. We finished the floors, doors, stairs, bathrooms, and when he left on Sept 6th 2012, twenty-three members of Renew came to stay for the weekend.

At this point, I had been alone for over ten years. That night a man I had met once, four months previously, arrived with the group. Before the weekend was over, I knew I wanted to see him again. I knew he was single. I also knew that I would have to make the move; he was worn out from destructive relationships.

The following Tuesday morning, I emailed him asking if I could talk to him some more. We talked for hours every day that week. Then one morning in my meditation, a voice said: "Ask him if he would help you run the place." I was shocked. I had made tentative arrangements before, with an American writer, to help me, but it had fallen through.

I was so disappointed, as I had hoped and had come to believe that something was beginning between us, but now all had changed. I knew I had to put the future of the house first. I asked him if he was interested, outlining what I had agreed with the American lady.

"Yes," he replied without a thought then said, "I was planning on moving anyway."

"Think about it," I said, "It will probably mean that we won't get together in any other way."

"Why can't we have both?" he replied.

He arrived two days later to look over the place and help me with the finishing touches. When he left at the weekend, I went with him knowing that I wanted both.

He moved in two weeks later. I can't say it has been easy, but I can say it has been wonderful. We are living in a world of learning and loving. We understand that everything that happens to us is part of a plan—a plan to help us to grow and move forward in life at a soul level.

My own journey has taught me that we have got to let go of our fear, our need to control both our own lives and the lives of others and to trust in something greater than ourselves which guides us along the way when we take the time to listen. Most of all, I have come to understand that our greatest teachers are sometimes the ones that have hurt us the most.

At the end of 2012, the fortieth anniversary of 1972 I realized that the most traumatizing incident in my life was not when a policewoman loaded a revolver with a single bullet, put the gun to my head and pulled the trigger repeatedly. It was, instead, at the end of 1972 when I decided I would kill if necessary to survive when yet another neighbour was murdered. I now realized that the most damage done to your soul is when you have destructive thoughts or actions towards another; however, the greatest growth is in supporting or helping others.

ABOUT MARY LYNCH

THE LONG ROAD HOME

This is a story of Mary Lynch's journey back to acknowledging the pain and terror of the youthful experiences in what was effectively a war zone. Only then could she heal and move on. Anyone who has ever suffered trauma will recognise and take solace from Mary's inspiring story.

Mary Lynch has endured a life of experiences some harrowing and others adventurous. All of which have guided her into becoming the inspirational leader she is today. Her insightful writing and wise approach to life has led Mary to becoming a popular and often controversial columnist in The Impartial Reporter newspaper.

Mary has been kind enough to share some of her writing in this book in our 'Collection of Articles'.

Since writing her story she has progressed further along her life's path. Mary's dream, determination and trust in the process of life has guided her towards manifesting her dream of creating a sanctuary for those who are in need. Ti Suaimhnis: House of Peacefulness was designed and built as a haven of peace and serenity in a troubled world.

"All are welcome here, whether to step out of the world for a time, to resolve an issue in your life, to deal with a crisis, or simply to enjoy the peace and beauty of this wild and remote area in the north-west of Ireland. This is a place where you can feel safe as you rest and recover"

Mary Lynch

MY CANCER STORY

A PERSONAL STORY SHARED BY EMILY SUN

It is December 2012. I went to see my specialist yesterday, and the news was good. There was no sign of cancer in my brain, and it was very unlikely there was any in my body.

I was first diagnosed with a rare type of lymphoma when I was thirty-three years old. Like many young women, the cancer was undetected until it was almost too late. As a young working mother, I was expected to feel tired. I had back, leg and hip pain from the lymphoma pushing on my nerves, but two doctors said that this was because I was carrying around my three-year-old son too much. I believed them because I was an otherwise healthy young mother and was able to do things like swim laps of the pool even when I was so tired and could barely breathe.

I knew something was seriously wrong when I went to get a full body massage and I felt worse afterwards. My face was puffy, and I had a bulging vein on the side of my neck. This is when I knew I had to go back to the doctor, who finally thought to order a blood test. That evening, the pathologist called me and told me to get straight to my nearest emergency department. That was July 23, 2010. No one ever forgets diagnosis day.

I went through six-hundred hours of

chemotherapy almost immediately and by the end of the year was declared in remission. I celebrated and moved on with my life. I threw myself into motherhood because I felt that I had missed out on so much time with my son. I picked up playing the violin again and started teaching my son's friends music. Then six months into remission, it started happening again. I had restless sleep, I felt tired, but this time I also felt nauseated and had headaches. I had random dizzy spells, sometimes when I was driving. These started at the end of my treatment but my specialist did not know much and dismissed these as migraines, post-treatment trauma, and he said to me when I tried to explain my symptoms in more detail, "If you had lymphoma in your head, you'd be dead by now!"

With this confident proclamation, my family and other doctors began to write off my symptoms as a side effect of my first treatment. Fortunately, my optometrist took my visual disturbances seriously, and within days of my specialist declaring me to be of perfect health, I found myself in ED again. This time, the scans picked up two large tumours at the back of my head on my occipital lobe.

It was happening again.

It was eerily similar to the first time I was diagnosed.

I was in the emergency department overnight with my husband, and no one slept. This time around, he wept.

Like the first time around, my instinct was to grab a pen and write a letter to my son to tell him all the things I thought I would not have a chance to say.

Unlike the first time, I was angry.

I was furious with my specialist for not listening to me and knew that even though I was sensitive to chemotherapy, a CNS relapse was not something that had a very good prognosis. At the time, I thought it had also returned to my body, and if this were the case, it meant I was in for very harsh treatment.

I knew I had to find a different specialist, one who knew the latest in lymphoma treatments, and that getting a good doctor would make all the difference to whether I lived or died.

I also remembered Shelsi, a girl from my on-line cancer support group, who had something similar happen to her. She went through very intensive treatment and radiotherapy, but she survived. She was four years out and had stopped interacting on the support forum. I knew that she had gone back to university, qualified as an early childhood teacher and was even working with children now. If they had the technology to cure her four years ago, surely there was something now.

I had to live. I didn't care how many medical

egos I hurt, but I knew I had to get out of the hospital I was at and get to someone who knew what they were doing. I had read enough cancer forums and memoirs to know that I had a curable cancer, even at late stage, and that the best chance one had was with a good doctor.

I emailed the young pharmacist who I knew might know where the brilliant young registrar from 2010 was. I tracked him down to his new job over East and told him what had happened. He calmed me down and told me the best thing to do was to go back to the first hospital I was treated at. I wasn't entirely convinced but remembered there was another specialist working there who played a big role in me getting the latest treatment the first time around. I called up the hospital and requested to switch to this more dynamic and personable young specialist. The day he agreed to be my doctor was the day I stopped writing what was my goodbye note to my son.

The hardest thing about getting sick in the first place was telling my son. He was only three years old at the time. We had a book called "Mom has cancer" that became his favourite book. People commented on how cute it was that he could read words like "cancer" and "chemotherapy". I felt guilty that he had to learn these words so early in life.

Getting sick again was difficult because there wasn't a book called "Mom has cancer again…" He had been with us at the last consultation when the specialist told me that I was fine.

"Dr Duck made a mistake," he said when my husband broke the news to him that I was sick again. "It was just a mistake."

This time around, I was treated in a quieter private hospital. I was advised against going to a private hospital the first time around because there was more staff around in a public hospital and there was no guarantee that you would see your specialist in a private hospital. But I was lucky. Dr A, my new specialist, was a talented and compassionate doctor who had a holistic approach to medicine, who knew how important gaining a patient's confidence was. While positive thoughts alone could not cure cancer, staying calm made getting through treatment easier. He reassured me he had a plan and a backup plan, and once I knew this, I could make the most of a bad situation.

The new hospital was like a hotel, and the food was real food. I took pleasure in ordering off the menu and requesting foods that I thought only my mother knew how to cook. These were just the frills of being in a private hospital, but they were the little things that kept me upbeat. I looked forward to photographing my café quality food and having my meals on ceramic plates.

Like the first time around, chemotherapy was continuous so I had to be an in-patient for a week at a time. In between my chemotherapy, I was always admitted for low blood counts and infection. I became weaker with each round but knew that I had to get through it. I saw friends when I was on chemo but asked them to visit me at times when I knew I had more energy. I didn't let anyone visit me when I was neutropenic, other than my husband, because I needed to get through therapy without delay. I knew that the cancer I had was aggressive and the treatment had to be aggressive. This time around, my specialist had the answers to every question I had about the disease and my treatment.

The first time around, the social worker at the hospital had helped me organize an in-home carer. My son hadn't started school at the time, so was discouraged from mixing too much with germ ridden children. I had been so tired leading up to diagnosis and I hadn't had a lot of time to do play dates, so I felt so guilty for leaving him in the company of a carer who seemed nice enough, but wasn't me.

After I got out of hospital after the first time, he told the carer to go away. He was happy never to see her again.

This second time around, we took a different approach. My condition was more critical, and the new hospital was a longer drive from home. My son had started school by the time of my relapse, and we had met some very good people in the school community. One of the mothers, Cathryn, was like a war general as she planned and organized a roster for my son. She made sure people on the list were people I trusted, and I was able to focus on my treatment knowing that my son was not socially isolated and was enjoying himself.

Afterwards, I saw good that had come out of such a terrible time. Not only was I able to focus on my treatment, he had a very sociable few months and learnt how to get along with different groups of people. I had become so insular over the two years because I was physically unwell, and it was good for him to go on day trips with other families and to spend time with other children. He picked up a love of painting, something he had done very little of, from spending time with Cathryn's very artistic family.

I stayed calm, because my doctor told me to, and did what I could to keep my spirits up. This was easy because one of the drugs that I was on induced mild euphoria. I was, however, still guilt ridden that I had fallen ill again. I had told my son that cancer was in the past and that mummy's hair was growing long again. Now my hair was falling out for the second time, and I had been told it would fall out again when I had to have whole head radiation.

At least I had treatment options, I reminded myself. I would deal with the luxury of living with side-effects afterwards. I knew that my doctor would not give me false hope, and he was optimistic about getting rid of the rogue lymphoma cells. Yet it was hard to not feel guilty about relapsing.

Rationally, I knew that there was nothing I could do about what fate threw at me; however, it was still very difficult coming to terms with the fact I had gotten sick in the first place. It helped that I had an on-line support group of other young people who had been stuck by this disease, yet it was difficult accepting that it was just bad luck.

The brain's primary function is to keep you safe and in having answers, there is the sense of security. If I did not step on the cracks, I would not have gotten sick. It was impossible not to engage in some magical thinking when you find yourself in this life threatening situation. I knew I had to stop torturing myself by trying to find some link between events I had control over and getting sick in the first place. There was a lot going on in my life when I was first diagnosed, but then again, most people have very full and slightly stressful lives in their early thirties. Not all of them had gotten lymphoma. What if it was because I hadn't eaten enough vegetables or hadn't eaten enough? Yet there were many anorexics and models in the world that were extremely underweight and never got cancer. What if I had travelled too much to places with toxic factories? What if I had used my brain too much in attempting to finish a post grad when breastfeeding? The longer the list grew, the more I was grasping at straws. In the end, I was too physically and mentally exhausted to care. It had happened. No one knew why in the same way no one knew why some people die in natural disasters and others survive.

After my chemotherapy treatment, I had to continue with twenty rounds of whole head cranial radiation. This scared me, as it would most people, because no one could really tell me what this treatment would do to me in the long term. They warned me about early dementia and permanent alopecia. Radiation is what we spend our lives trying to avoid even though we are exposed to it in small doses on a daily basis.

I did not want my head radiated twenty times. People reassured me that chemotherapy was more difficult and just as toxic. But I knew that it was my best chance of survival and to prevent a relapse. The side effect of radiation was life, and whilst no one could reassure me how much life I would get, I realized that neither did healthy people.

I made it through the rest of my treatment and, at the time of writing, am expected to live. I celebrate not being dead, because I know how close I came both times. My son also understands this. Yesterday (Dec 2012), I had a follow up consult with Dr A, and I called my son straight away with the news that I was still in remission.

"So has Doctor A has gotten all the cancer out?" he asked. He is only five, but he understands that every cell has to be killed and that rogue dormant cells could trigger a relapse. I wish I didn't have to teach him the basics of oncogenesis at five years old, but he is a bright child, and it is easier to explain the science.

He has raised the very abstract concept of death with me. He has from time to time asked me if I nearly died. I say, "Yes, but I'm okay now." Then he will reassure himself by repeating, "Gong gong (grandfather) will die first, then po po (grandmother)." Then he'll say, "You know Dad will die before you because you are younger."

I can't bring myself to say, "Well maybe not. You never know," because he is only a five-year-old despite his advance verbal skills.

We have also explained to him that he will not have a younger brother and sister because the chemotherapy killed all of mummy's eggs. He knows that he was made from an egg and will sometimes say, "Mum, am I the only egg you had left?"

To say that it was hard to lose my fertility because of treatment is an understatement. I have often tried to mitigate the grief by saying that it is entirely possible that I would have chosen to have the one child, but I know that this is not true. In these moments where I think about the losses, I remind myself of what I have. There are women younger than me who have been through more intense treatment who will never have a biological child. There are women older than me who have never had cancer who will never have a child. There are women my age who will go through early menopause even without cancer treatment. This is life.

Nearly three years on from my initial diagnosis, I am hoping to put this bad experience behind me. I am so mentally and physically exhausted from the journey that I try not to think too much about what happened. I see a psychologist on a regular basis who helps me accept what has happened and move on with my life. There is no point waiting for the next deluge that may or may not come, as it is much more pleasurable to enjoy the warmth of the sun.

I have yet to return to my life from before I got sick, and I'm not sure if I ever will. I always go back to a quote by Joseph Campbell which reminds us, "We must be willing to let go of the life we planned so as to have the life that is waiting for us." I don't really know what life is out there for me, but I am just very grateful that I have the chance to find out.

About Emily Sun

Unfortunately Emily's cancer journey still continues: Shortly after writing this story for us she was given the devastating news that her cancer had returned. Since then she has been on another harrowing crusade to stay alive.

Even though she is so ill, this inspiring woman has created quite a positive stir by doing everything within her power to increase awareness about the lack of registered Asian stem cell donors that there are in the world.

Utilising her contacts and the goodwill of everyone who wants to help; she has successfully appeared on Weekend Sunrise, on the cover of a Japanese magazine, has had a strong presence on YouTube, facebook and twitter as well as requesting on an individual level that every single Asian person she knows consider registering, this will not only benefit her quest it will benefit the needs of others in a similar situation.

We do hope that in the not so near future we will be sharing a happy ending to Emily's story. We hope that Emily fulfils her dream of watching her son grow up – something that many of us take for granted.

If you or anyone you know is of Asian origin take a moment to visit **www.emilyneedsstemcells.com** and consider becoming a donor and passing the details on to someone you know. Together we all can make a difference.

All for a Reason

A LIFE JOURNEY SHARED BY CHRISTIE LYONS

I was a painfully shy child, and I was often mistaken for being rude or not even noticed at all. Even though I felt I had so much to give, I didn't have the confidence to let it out. I really feel that I have come full circle in my thirty-odd years: from being someone that was scared to utter a word to someone I didn't feel completely comfortable with, to now not only being in a leadership position in my career but writing this story about my life so far.

I do truly believe that the events I have experienced in my life have given me the confidence I so desperately needed, and although I have had some challenging times, I know that each and every moment of my life has happened for a reason and has taught me a life lesson.

I have always wondered what it would be like to document some of the events of my life. I often tell people when I first meet them how I could 'write a story about my life' and have often considered doing so but never really felt that push to actually do it, nor felt that anyone would be interested in it. Recently however, I received a nudge in a kind email I received from a beautiful person I met on the internet, and the warm, fuzzy feeling I got at the prospect of writing about my journey so far, made me feel like I just needed to do it once and for all.

When I was in primary school, I'd talk about how I was going to be a writer one day, and I always received support and encouragement from my teachers and family in regards to my writing, which pushed me to do it even more—writing poems and short stories. Somehow though, along the way, that childhood dream got lost and my writing was limited to my personal journal. Any creativity in the process was lost.

I'm not quite sure how or why I stopped writing, but I did find other passions eventually. It took me a while though and I finally found what it was I wanted to do. It was worth the wait, and I do believe wholeheartedly that everything that has happened throughout my life has led me to the love of my work and is also the reason why I seem to have this knack of seeing the positives in life.

I do sometimes receive comments like, "Wow you handled that well", or "You were so strong in that situation", which I found odd, because in fact, not so long ago, I felt quite weak and it actually made me angry to think that people thought I was 'strong' emotionally. I would think, "Are you mad? If only you knew how much I cried in private and what went through my mind…you wouldn't say I was strong then." But now I realise that in spite of all of that, I was in fact strong, and I still am, and that's why I'm now often able to see the positives in things.

Admittedly, I don't necessarily feel strong all the time, nor do I feel like I need to, but I must admit, at times when I would expect myself to break down, I surprise myself more and more every day and realise that I must be gaining even more strength as my journey continues. I'm not ashamed to admit that I suffer from depression and anxiety, and I believe that being able to talk about it is the key to managing the illness. And so, this leads me to my life so far.

Memories of my early childhood always make me smile, and I think it's because my mother and I lived with my grandparents for the first five years of my life. Nan and Pa's house was always my 'safe place' even right up until a few years ago. The house in the suburbs of Melbourne was one that my grandparents had bought in the 50's before my mum was born and although it wasn't anything fancy, to me it was and always will be 'home', and I loved everything about it. The memories that were made in that home will remain with me for the rest of my life, and a few years ago when my grandparents sold it, it broke my heart.

My mum fell pregnant with me at the age of seventeen, and she raised me with the help of my grandparents in their home until I was five years old. I remember those years to be some of the happiest of my life. My Pa would tell me stories, always got involved in all my pretend games, and basically, in my eyes, was my 'Dad'. This relationship continued to be a father–daughter type relationship all throughout my childhood and adult years, and I will be grateful for his wisdom and support for the rest of my life. My Nan was, and still is, my rock. She took care of me when I was sick, disciplined me when I needed it (and still does), and is such a strong, beautiful woman.

When I was about six years old, Mum married a man who, in all honesty, was not the brightest of people and to top it off, had a drinking problem. My baby brother Jim was born in 1986 and has been one of my closest friends since, even though he is seven years my junior. Mum's marriage with this man didn't last long, and we were back and living near my grandparents before long, after he hurt my brother in one of his many drunken episodes and Mum had decided enough was enough.

Mum, Jim and I spent several years living in a two bedroom flat right around the corner from my grandparent's house, which was handy because whenever I had a tantrum or an argument with Mum, I could run around to Nan and Pa's house and it was like 'running away' even though I was completely safe. It made me feel better anyway. A lot of what I remember from those years of my life was that Mum worked a lot, and so Jim and I still spent quite a bit of time at our grandparent's house.

The fact that my brother and I had to share a bedroom for all those years wasn't ideal, but that's all Mum could afford and we had to make do. I remember trying one day to rearrange the furniture in our room so that we could have 'separate sides', but the room just wasn't big enough. Plus, although my little brother was a pain most of the time during those years, come night time, I would coax him up into my top bunk so that I could give him a cuddle—more for my sake than his, as it made me feel safe.

After having such a promising and supportive primary school experience, I got the shock of my life moving into high school. I was withdrawn for one thing, and that didn't help me at all in making friends or socialising in any way. I did manage to find myself a small group of friends that stood by me through high school and helped me have a few laughs and get into some mischief along the way.

It was on one of our regular sleepovers that my girlfriends and I got onto the subject of my father. I had explained to them earlier on how I had never met my father before, and the only details I had were his name and where he went to high school. I guess it was just one of those subjects that I had not really thought about overly much because I had never known what it was like to have my father around. My Pa was my dad as far as I was concerned, and that was enough for me. But as time went on, curiosity got the better of me, and we started fishing through the phone book for his name. Well, there were hundreds of them! We tried a couple of numbers with no luck, but then one stood out to me. I asked my girlfriend to call for me, so she did. She asked him a couple of questions to make sure we had the right person, and then we hung up, freaking out that we were pretty sure my father was just on the other end of the line.

After this phone call, questions started niggling away at me: Who was he? Did I look like him? Why didn't Mum ever talk about him? I felt scared, nervous, and angry. So I asked my Nan. To this day, I couldn't tell you why I didn't just go to my mum and ask her, but I didn't. After telling Nan details about what my girlfriends and I had done the night before, Nan seemed confused and angry. She wasn't angry at me but at my mum, which I found strange in itself. This is when I found out that not only had Mum lied about the whole situation to my Nan but also that my mum had never actually told my father she was pregnant. All this time, my father was out there, and he had no idea that I even existed.

That night, when Mum got home from work, Nan confronted her about the situation. This led to Mum calling my father herself to tell him he had a thirteen year old daughter. I didn't get to hear the conversation Mum had with him on the phone, but she did tell me when she hung up that I had a little sister and that my father agreed to come and meet me on the proviso that a blood test be done to prove it.

I remember the day I met my father for the first time very clearly. I was running late from an after school activity and when I got home and walked in the door, it was like looking at myself. I looked so much like him, and he later told my mum that he no longer needed a blood test because he knew I was his daughter just by looking at me. I honestly don't remember any of the other conversations that were had that afternoon, but I do remember instantly feeling that I had somehow missed out on a whole lot. After all, this whole other half of my life had been missing and I knew nothing about it. I also had a sister, and who knows how many other family members!

I ended up meeting with my father every few months or so, but each outing or visit was extremely awkward, what with my bashfulness and also the fact that his wife must have felt quite uncomfortable in my presence. When I was sixteen, I gained another sister when he and his wife had their second daughter. It was not long after she was born that I lost touch with him for several years.

Around the same time I met my father, my mum started a new relationship with Benjamin, who also had three children of his own. One of them was in the same high school as me, although she was one year my senior and I only knew her by name. His other two children were slightly younger than my brother and I, and in them, we each found two very close friends as well as step-siblings. When Benjamin asked Mum to move in with him a couple of years later, my brother and I finally got our own rooms, and something so simple to some was a godsend to us, especially me, being a teenage girl.

Benjamin was a quiet man, and although we sometimes clashed and I thought he was grumpy so much of the time, he was there and was the only male influence I had other than my grandfather. He was a constant in my teenage years, and I guess I just took for granted that he was in my life. When I look back now I wonder if I'd tried harder, whether I may have had a more fulfilling relationship with him; nonetheless, I was a teenager, and my focus was on my friends and new-found social life. So, my mum and step-dad took a backburner.

Moving into our new house meant that I was no longer embarrassed to have friends over, and so I started socialising a little more as I got older. I also met a boy at school who adored me, and without even thinking, I jumped at any chance to be in a relationship. I ended up marrying this boy just before my 21st birthday. Being so young and naïve, I hadn't necessarily thought the decision through completely. I was desperate for security and someone to take care of me, and it was just the 'next step' in our relationship. I had also developed a wonderful relationship with his family, and seeing as my relationship with my own mother wasn't so great lately, it filled a void in my life by being close with his Mum instead.

Our wedding was a traditional one, and it was beautiful, but even though it was a memorable day, I had a feeling even then that it wasn't going to last. I simply didn't feel that magic that I expected to feel when I got married, and I honestly could not see myself spending the rest of my life with him, but I did it anyway because I thought that I would never find anyone else that would love me.

We honeymooned on the Gold Coast, and on our first night, we arranged a special dinner for two in a revolving restaurant overlooking the coast. This was a night that will remain imprinted in my memory for the rest of my life. Half way through dinner, one of the waiters came over to us, letting me know that I had a phone call. A feeling of dread came over me instantly, and I couldn't explain why. I took the phone call, and it was my mum, asking me to go to our room and call her.

We left the restaurant immediately. All the way down in the elevator, I worried that something had happened to Benjamin. Two days before, at our wedding reception, Benjamin had danced with me and hugged me tight and said, "I love you." This was something he had never done in all the eight years he'd been in our lives, and something in my heart told me that things weren't right.

As soon as we walked into our hotel room I called my mum, and as she said the words, it was as if I already knew what she was going to say. All I remember is passing the phone straight to my new husband and running into the bathroom to throw up after she said the words: "It's Benjamin. He committed suicide today."

I just wanted to be home, but the earliest flight we could get was the next morning. That night on the Gold Coast, I was filled with terror, and I hope that I never have to experience a night like that again. Coming home was even more terrifying for me; seeing Mum and the horror on her face after having found him dead in her car, holding her photo the day before. I have never seen my mum look that way before, and I could see how haunted she was.

Benjamin had written and left a letter addressed to my mum just before he died, and amongst all his heart-breaking words that he left for her, he also wrote a message for my brother and I apologising for what he had done. I remember feeling so angry at him for doing this to my mum. I was also angry for the pain this had caused my brother, because he had looked up to him and Benjamin was his father figure for so many years. I had a mixture of so many feelings: anger, sadness, fear.

Just a couple of days after Benjamin died, I was told to sort through my old bedroom to clear out what I wanted to keep because Mum wanted to be out of the house as soon as possible. I remember feeling so terrified, sick and faint as I walked into the house and felt his presence everywhere. I grabbed a few things from my room but couldn't do it for very long because the feeling was so overwhelming, and it made me sick. I remember focussing on things that I used to see every day but somehow stood out to me now: the car that he gassed himself in, the chair that he spent so much time in putting bets on the horses on a Saturday morning, and the kitchen table where he was sitting just a few days before chatting to me as I raced around organising last minute details the night before my wedding day. So many things raced through my mind, and I had to get out of there. As quick as a flash, all the great memories of my wedding day, my honeymoon and even the memories I had made in that house through my teens had been blocked out by something in my mind that now felt it was all too hard to comprehend.

After the funeral, I went back to what I had been doing for the past year and avoided my mum as much as I could, mostly because I felt back then that we didn't have anything in common and Benjamin's suicide just made things even harder on our relationship. I noticed myself becoming more and more resentful of my mum when I thought about my own father and how she had deprived me of the chance to know him, and now, my brother and I had lost our step-dad too.

It was around this time that I decided to try and reach out to my father again in the hope that he would somehow magically want to 'be my dad' after hearing of the news. I did manage to squeeze in a couple of visits in the following months and got to see my now fourteen-year-old eldest sister and my younger sister who had not long since turned five years old. Again, visiting them did not have the effect I'd quite hoped for, and all it did was give me feelings of jealousy, making me wonder why my sisters were lucky enough to have him in their lives every day and I never got the chance.

Once again, my dreams were shot at hoping to have a relationship with my dad, and after trying to keep in regular contact, he was always too busy and so I shut it out again for a while and got on with my new married life.

Once my new husband and I had bought our own home, things started to settle down, and I started forming closer relationships with some friends at work. I found myself having a lot in common with one girl, who had moved down from the country and needed somewhere to stay. I invited her to stay with my husband and I, and I was excited when she accepted my offer as she gave me a distraction from the awkwardness I was feeling at home with my husband; deep down part of me knew our relationship was not going to last much longer.

As hard as I tried not to, I also found myself falling for a guy I worked with, James. He was a little younger than me, but we just clicked and got along really well. I also felt something that I hadn't felt in the seven years I had been with my husband, having been with him since I was fifteen years old.

I'd somehow gained a new-found confidence; he would tell me I was beautiful and made me feel like I was my age again. After all, at this point in my life, I was still only 22 years old and wanted all of a sudden to have fun!

One weekend away with my new best friend and my husband, after having stressed myself out immensely for a couple of months trying to find a way to tell my high school sweetheart and new husband that I wanted a divorce, suddenly I found the courage. I just blurted it out. I gathered from his reaction that this outburst of mine was unexpected, and he broke down. I felt an enormous amount of guilt but also an overwhelming feeling of relief. It was as if I felt free for the first time in my life, and I felt like anything was a possibility; the world was my oyster. Amongst all the chaos of my announcement, I did find it odd that my best friend was consoling my now ex-husband, and not me, but I didn't care at that point. All I wanted to do was start living my life.

The drive home from that weekend trip was one of the longest of my life, and I was actually scared that he was going to crash, he was that angry. The minute I got home, he told me to leave, and so I drove to my mum's house nearby. My brother, being only 16 at the time, answered the door with a cricket bat as my mum was overseas and it was two in the morning. The minute he saw my face, however, he dropped the bat and hugged me as I let it all out and confided in my little brother.

Although the next two weeks were painful as I came to the realisation of the decision I had just made, it was also one of the most liberating times of my life, where I realised I was in charge of my life. I was 23 and single for the first time since I was 15 years old. You would think that I would have made the most of it, but no, not me. Insecure and impatient, I decided to jump straight into another serious relationship just three days after my separation. I fell straight into the arms of my friend from work. He was attracted to me; that's all I needed. That was my pre-requisite for a relationship back then. Never mind whether I really thought he was relationship material, whether he had the same goals in life as I did, any of the important stuff. All that mattered to me was that he wanted me.

I felt a lot of guilt for being in another serious relationship so soon after my separation and my ex-husband's family let me know what they thought of me once they found out. I was made to feel like I was irresponsible, immature and completely in the wrong for making the decision to leave my husband. Soon after I'd moved out, I'd asked my best friend if she would consider moving in with me, and when she told me that she'd prefer to continue living with my husband, it was pretty obvious that there was a lot more to the story than I first knew. I'd been naïve enough to hand over nearly everything I'd owned, including my house, because I felt guilty that I was the one to instigate the split, but it turned out that my ex-husband was just fine without me. They are happily married today with two children, and my guilt about the situation dissipated very quickly.

James and I got along fantastically, as we had done at work. He also introduced me to some life-long friends, whom I still have a relationship with today, and they taught me what a real friendship is. This amazing group of friends had stuck by each other for years and were more like a family than a bunch of mates. Through James, I was lucky enough to become a part of this 'family', and for that I will be forever grateful.

These new friends became such a big part of my life, and seeing as we all lived relatively close by, our home became a meeting place and somewhere that everyone hung out at all times of the day and night. It was over this time that I came to know them all so very well and grew to love each of them very quickly. Two of these friends in particular, who were also best mates themselves, made their way close to my heart as I spent more and more time with them. Dave was someone who understood me on a level that no one ever had before and had a way of making me feel special. Anthony and I got along like we were siblings. He often came to me for advice about his own relationship and was frequently protective of me.

This group of friends had a very strong influence over me, and although we were all relatively young, they provided on-going support and guidance to me during one of the most important times of my life. One of these friends in particular, Ethan, is still someone that I seek guidance from in times when I am lost and have no answers.

The relationship between James and I was quite a short-lived one in retrospect, all of two and a half years long, but that relationship I rushed into was for a reason, maybe one of the most important ones of my life, because he gave me the love of my life: my son.

Hamish was born in 2003, five weeks premature, and my labour was a very easy, natural one. He was, however, kept in the special care nursery for a week after I gave birth, and this may have contributed to me suffering from postnatal depression. It wasn't until Hamish was about three months old that I finally bonded with him and the guilt I felt from that remained with me for several years. At the time, in those first few months, I didn't feel much at all. I just got on with the routine of things but never really felt overly much towards Hamish. I was happy to leave him with anyone to babysit and wasn't interested in just 'being' with him. It wasn't until he was about three months old that I fell asleep with him in my arms one night on the couch and woke up to have this revelation all of a sudden that I was his Mum! It was then that I realised how much I was in love with this little man, and ever since then, I have tried my very hardest to be the very best Mum I can be. I do believe that I have been.

James, Hamish and I lived with my mum and brother, and so the help we received from them while Hamish was a baby was amazing. Mum loved being a grandparent and having us live with her made her happy. My brother, while only 17 years old, took the role of Uncle Jim quite seriously and doted on his new nephew. As much as Mum and Jim were a great support to me, I couldn't really say the same for James. He was young and immature and unfortunately hadn't quite grasped the concept of being a responsible father yet.

It was during this time that I became a lot closer to Dave. He supported me through postnatal depression and being a new Mum. Dave helped me with midnight feeds, let me sleep when he knew I was exhausted, and made me feel good about myself when I felt down. That was exactly what I needed at such a complicated time in my life, and he made me feel as though everything just felt right when he was around. I felt as though I had known him all my life and he understood me in a way that no one else had ever done before.

Over those few months, Dave and I got to know each other on such a deeper level, and we shared our fears, our hopes and dreams, and opened our hearts. All we needed to do was look into each other's eyes and know what the other was feeling; I was falling in love, but I couldn't come out and say it in so many words because I knew it could never happen. Those months were some of the happiest of my life but also heart-breaking at the same time. I had fallen in love and knew deep down that it was real but also knew that it couldn't happen unless I wanted to risk my relationship with James, and risk my son's relationship with his father. Every time I saw Dave, it was a struggle, and it ate away at my heart every day we couldn't be together.

James and I separated just after Hamish's first birthday, and this time, I didn't feel as liberated. I knew it was the right thing to do, but it also scared me to think that I might lose my new 'family' and I genuinely wanted for James and I to remain friends; not only for our son's sake, but I really did cherish his friendship. It must have been destined because we are still very close friends to this day, and I am once again very grateful for that. It has also meant that our son has seen that although his Mum and Dad's relationship didn't work, we do genuinely love each other as friends, and that means so much to me.

After James and I separated, I continued to watch Dave move on with his life, and it hurt so much that eventually I decided that I needed to do something to distract myself. I couldn't handle it, and so I started chatting with men online. Once again, I fell into the same old habit of getting into a relationship without thinking, all because he showed interest in me, but this time, I still had Dave in the back of my mind the entire time. I knew that I would never get over him and knew that in order for me to move on with my life, I had to get away from him, as much as it hurt me to do it.

I packed my life up, along with Hamish's, who was now 18 months old, and moved to Geelong. We moved into a small unit close to the beach, and it was just the two of us. We lived on our own for nearly a year, and this time helped me to make up for the bonding time that I'd missed when he was first born. We did everything together, just simple things like going down to the local beach, hanging out at the park, and going for walks. In between this time, we spent more and more time with my new boyfriend and his young daughter. It was during this time that I decided I wanted to make more of my life, and I made the decision to go back to school.

I started studying early childhood education full time, and after going to classes for the first week, I decided that this was what I was meant to do all along. I loved it already, and I hadn't even started working in the field yet. This was an 'Aha' moment where I had finally found something in my life that made sense. I was happy, making the most of my life, and starting something I knew was going to be life-changing for me. I felt proud of myself and knew that my family would be proud as well.

It was during my first year of study, and after about six months of living away from all my family and friends, that I received another one of those phone calls that will remain in my memory forever. The phone call was from Hamish's aunty. "There's been a car accident" was the first thing I heard, and I instantly thought that James had been hurt. She reassured me that he was okay and proceeded to tell me that although James had been in the car and was badly injured and in hospital, another very dear friend, Anthony, had died early that morning. I had never felt more homesick.

That day, I drove back to Melbourne with a million things going through my mind. Anthony was a very dear friend of mine, and I was grieving for him but at the same time, I found myself thinking of Dave. Dave had been in the car with Anthony, and he had watched him die. How I wished more than ever that I could just be there for him and comfort him during such a tragic time of his life. He had just lost his best friend, and I couldn't even attempt to ease his pain.

I arrived at the hospital, and when I walked in and saw James, I instantly burst into tears. One of my best friends, and the father of my child, had been lucky enough to live through this horrific accident, but he looked terrible. As I stood by his bed and he told me details about the accident, I started to feel weak. Between looking at him all beaten and bruised and dealing with the shock of such a sudden tragic death, I felt all of a sudden like I was going to collapse. I had to leave, as the magnitude of it all sunk in for me.

Anthony's funeral was tragic, yet beautiful. As expected, the church was filled with people who knew and loved him. I felt sick as I arrived at the church, and it was as if I was not only feeling my own grief but also each time I looked at Dave, I felt so much pain for him; it killed me to not be able to just hold him while he cried. I also felt guilty for moving away six months ago and wondered if I could have been there for them all had I stayed in Melbourne.

A few months later, Hamish and I went to the airport to say goodbye to his Daddy as he was leaving to live interstate for his recent acceptance into the Navy. What was supposed to have been a short-term move to support James's career change eventually turned into a permanent relocation, and Hamish's relationship with his dad has been a long distance one ever since. Although this meant that for several years I was his only parent and sole influence, I have always reminded Hamish how much his father adores him and have actively encouraged and supported their relationship to remain positive as Hamish has gotten older.

When I graduated from Tafe in 2006, I was offered a full time teaching position straight away, and I loved it from the very first day I started. This small childcare centre became my second home, and I even enrolled Hamish into my kinder group for his final year before school. While I became more and more engrossed in my work, it also boosted my confidence to places I had never imagined possible. Working with children ignited a passion in me that I never knew existed, and it strengthened my forever growing bond with my son as I soaked in the magnificence of everything he was learning, right alongside him.

I realised very quickly that this new job of mine was not just a career choice but yet another turning point in my life. It genuinely made me happy and made me feel like I was doing something worthwhile, and it wasn't long before I was promoted to director of the centre. I came to the realisation soon after that I had been jumping from one relationship to the next over the last fourteen years all because I'd believed that I had to be in a relationship to be happy. With the joy I was receiving from being a Mum and my career progression, I finally felt that I was ready to go at it alone.

Once again, I found myself packing my things up and moving Hamish and I into our own house again. This was a time in my life that scared me and excited me all at the same time. I was free again, but this time I was looking forward to being single because for the first time in my life, I felt confident, attractive and successful. Now, I may have overdone it a bit, but I did have a lot of fun in 2008. Every chance I got, I travelled, I went out drinking and dancing, and to put it politely, made the most of being single. When I look back now, I realise I was quite irresponsible and perhaps a bit immature, but I just had to get it out of my system. After all, I had never been in a position where I could just have fun on a night out and not worry about answering to anyone.

At this stage, Hamish was in his first year of primary school, and although I was enjoying my single life, I was also riddled with guilt at all the upheaval I had caused him from exposing him to so many changes in his young life. I made a concerted effort to make sure that I continued to spend as much quality time with Hamish as I could, and I also made the decision to always be honest with him and instil in him the importance of talking about his feelings. Even now, Hamish knows that he can come to me for anything and that I will always be here to talk about anything that is on his mind. Although Hamish is quite a sensitive soul, he is also the most thoughtful, kind and compassionate person I have ever known. I must have done something right.

In late 2008, with Hamish and I still enjoying our lives in Geelong, someone very special to me made his way back into my life. Dave and I had seen and spoken to each other on the odd occasion over the years, but it was only ever in passing. After three years of hardly any contact, I had forced him to the back of my mind to ease my heartache for him, and when he first started wanting to catch up with me after that long, I tried to push him away. I told myself that I couldn't go through that heartbreak again; it had taken me far too long for me to recover the first time around. Dave persisted, and I decided that I would allow him into my life again, but I was determined not to allow my feelings to get the better of me. It scared me way too much because I knew deep down how much I loved him and still knew that a relationship for us wasn't a possibility. My feelings, however, started to get the better of me very quickly.

Dave and I chatted online and over text messages, talking about the past and present. The more we spoke and spent time together, the more his feelings for me started to show. Dave opened up and let me know he had feelings for me, and that he had for many years, but he knew they couldn't be acted on because of James. Deep down I already knew this, but it was finally nice to hear him say it. The tricky part was James. Dave and James were still friends, and we both knew that nothing could ever eventuate without the risk of upsetting him.

My very first trip abroad was booked in early 2009, and I was flying to Thailand alone. I was due to meet a friend I had met on the internet over there, and in the months leading up to the trip, Dave and I spent more and more time together while we could, each of us knowing that it would eventually have to stop before we fell too deep again. We agreed that we would spend one more night together before I left for my overseas trip, but that after that, we would have to go back to being friends before we caused each other too much pain.

That last night was one of the most beautiful of my life. When Dave looked into my eyes, it was as if he was looking right into my soul when he said, "I do love you, you know." At that moment, I felt like I would fall apart. I felt all my love for him, all the pain, and every single feeling I'd felt for him over the last six years come flooding back. I was so confused.

My trip to Thailand was another one of those times in my life that made it change forever. For one thing, it was a miracle in itself that I managed to survive an overseas flight by myself, being the nervous wreck that I once was, but I got through it and felt so proud of myself when I arrived. The culture in Thailand was fascinating to me, and it opened my eyes immediately to the fact that I wanted to see more of the world.

I couldn't get Dave out of my mind the whole trip, and every moment I could, I called or emailed him, and I texted him regularly every day. One afternoon on a ferry to Phi Phi Island, I was lying on the top deck of the boat, getting a tan and listening to my iPod, when a song came on that I had dubbed 'Our Song' because Dave had sung it to me all those years ago when we first fell in love. I paused the song and texted him to play it too so we could 'listen to it together'. He told me he would, and as I lay there on the boat, I listened to the song and realised that I couldn't live without him.

Phi Phi island was beautiful, and I felt completely at peace while I was there. I was walking along the beach while the sun was coming down one evening and my phone beeped. I checked it, and a message from Dave told me that he had sent me an email and he'd wanted me to read it as soon as I could. I couldn't get to an internet café from where

I was, and so I asked him to explain. Dave then proceeded to tell me that he although he knew we'd agreed to just be friends when I got home, his feelings for me were too strong and he wanted us to give it a shot. I don't think I'd smiled so much in my life as I did after that message, and I didn't waste any time in telling him I felt exactly the same way.

Our relationship moved very quickly after that, and we just couldn't get enough of each other. It was as if we were making up for all the years of lost time; after all, we had been in love for six years before we finally made it together. Our lives together made perfect sense and everything just fell into place like it was meant to be. Even when it came time for us to tell James about our relationship, it was much easier than we thought, and he was genuinely happy for us. Dave told me how he had not felt this much happiness in such a long time, and it was the first time he felt like his life had purpose since he lost his best friend four years earlier.

The three of us eventually moved back to Melbourne after my job situation changed, and I'm so glad that we did because I realised how much I'd missed, living so far away from my family. I managed to secure a similar position in a Melbourne childcare centre and am still there now and loving it. Moving back home has allowed me to rekindle my relationships with my family, and even though I had maintained contact with them all while I was in Geelong, it was never the same as being close by.

Our relationship has not been easy, and there have been many tears along the way. When we had both settled into our relationship and what I call the 'butterflies stage' started to wear off, each of our pasts started to come to the surface. It was as if we could both finally relax and breathe, and once we did, all of the pain, stress and heartache we'd both experienced tapped us on the shoulder and said, 'Hey, remember me?'

Thankfully, we were both brave enough to seek some help, even though it took a while for each of us to acknowledge that either of us had been suffering from depression. By opening up and talking about our pasts, it has helped us to work through some of the struggles, challenges and pain that we have been through, and it has also made our relationship so much stronger.

With both Dave and I suffering from depression at the same time, it has definitely had its challenges, but not once has one of us waivered from the commitment that we made to be together. If anything, the fact that we are both still as much in love with each other, if not more, than we were when we first fell in love, again makes me believe that everything happens for a reason.

Part of my healing was to confront some of my fears, and one of those fears was opening up to my father. After seeing how much pain I was in by not having a relationship with him, Dave was the one who pushed me to talk to him about how I was feeling. It took me a while to gather the courage to do this, and finally one day at work, I just broke down into tears and decided to call him. He must have heard the panic in my voice and told me to come over straight away. As soon as I walked in the door, I burst into tears and handed him a letter I had written to him. I knew that I wouldn't have been able to talk with him in person about how I really felt, and so I had written all my feelings on paper months before and carried it around with me until that day.

The outcome of that visit with my father seemed promising initially; however, our relationship really hasn't grown since then, nor has it improved. There is a difference though now. I no longer let the fact that we don't have a 'father–daughter relationship' bother me. I had the courage to tell him how I felt; I opened my heart to my father, and I cannot do any more than that. In my mind, I have 'let go' of the problem and the pain that I felt about not knowing him as a child, and I have been honest in how I felt about it all to him. I knew when I spoke to him that what he did with the information was his decision, and it still is. I do still have limited contact with my father from time to time; however, I have truly let go of the hope of ever having a close relationship with him.

During that meeting with my father, I came to another important realisation. I realised that I was very angry at my mum. I didn't fully recognise or acknowledge my anger until that day, but when I did, it hit me like a ton of bricks. It upset me that I was feeling that way about my mum, but it also gave me a bit of relief because it explained a lot of the anxiety I had been experiencing and the reasoning behind why we didn't have much of a relationship anymore. I needed to confront my mum as well, but I knew I wasn't ready to take that step yet.

I spent several months avoiding contact with Mum because I felt way too much anger at her, and honestly just didn't feel like speaking to her for a while. I also didn't like the fact that she had isolated herself over the years from not only me but the rest of our family, and I knew that I wouldn't be able to open up to her until I was completely ready.

That day came when she was at my grandparents' house one Sunday afternoon, and they had been prompting me to talk to her. I sat her down and just blurted it all out. It felt odd because it was almost as if our roles had been reversed, and I was her mother, giving her a bit of tough love. I told her how angry I was at her and asked her what she was thinking when she denied me the chance to have my father in my life. I let it all out, and I didn't censor anything. I confronted her about her self-isolation from her family, my brother and I in particular, and told her how I felt I didn't even have a Mum at the moment. Mum ended up breaking down, which was difficult for me to see, but she gave me the answers I had needed for so long, and it gave me instant relief that I had finally gotten all my feelings off my chest.

Just a few weeks later, in August 2011, my Pa had a massive stroke. He fought it though, which allowed us to spend the following two weeks saying goodbye to him. It didn't take long for all of our family members to make it into the hospital, and we gathered together for support as we always do. After Pa had been through surgery, we were allowed to visit him in ICU for brief moments, so I took Hamish in with me to see him. Pa had tubes all over him, and his mouth was tied open tightly so he could breathe. It was not an ideal situation for an eight-year-old to be experiencing, but I didn't know whether or not this might be his only opportunity to say goodbye. Hamish and I told him we loved him, as I tried my hardest to explain the situation honestly with my little boy.

The following morning Pa was awake, and as I walked in, he was playing with the sheet with his hand. I went over to him, gave him a kiss and said hello, and he lifted up his hand, cupped my left cheek in his hand, and smiled at me. It was such a beautiful moment that I will remember forever. Hamish read to him and showed him a card he had made for him that morning, with a photo pasted of the two of them on the front. Pa watched Hamish intently as he read it to him. Pa held onto both mine and Hamish's hands together, squeezing our hands in his. Hamish started crying, and as I was trying to console him, Pa was looking at us. He continued to squeeze Hamish's hand, and then he pinched him, which made us laugh. I'm convinced he did that to stop us from crying because he'd always hated seeing people cry.

Those two weeks were quite possibly the hardest of my life. Mum and I spent a lot of time with him in the hospital at night times, once everyone else had been in to see him for the day. I felt exhausted and emotionally drained, but I kept going in because I wanted to make the most of what time Pa had left with us. I found that the more time we spent at the hospital, the less sad I felt, and slowly the sadness faded and I started to feel at peace.

One night when we were there, Pa kept looking at the both of us to see if we were still there. At one point, he was finding it hard to breathe, and Mum asked him, "Are you finding it hard to breathe?" Pa nodded, then looked at me and shook his head. Mum asked, "Are you sure? Is it hard to breathe?" He nodded. I told him, "You don't need to pretend Pa, I'm a big girl." Mum added, "She's a smart girl, she gets it from you." I believe that the time Mum and I spent with Pa in those two weeks was not only for us to say goodbye to him, but was also an opportunity for Mum and I to bond again. Although Pa was unable to speak, I could tell in his eyes and the way he looked at us that he had seen us reconnect as well.

Pa was moved into his own private room after a little while, and it was much nicer as we were able to spend time with him as a family. Dave had been and bought Pa an Essendon Bombers teddy and throw rug for his bed that day, and when I showed Pa, he threw his arm up in the air above his head as if to say, "Yes!" But after that, he held his arm over his eyes and turned away. I started stroking Pa's head, while telling Hamish, "When I was a little girl, Pa used to stroke my head like this to get me to sleep. Didn't you Pa?" Pa nodded.

I felt so much admiration for him that night. I said to him, "You're amazing." He shook his head, and I replied, "Yes you are." He shook his head again. I leaned closer and whispered, "You are. You've been like my dad. You've taught me everything." He laid back then and closed his eyes. I then told Pa that I wasn't scared anymore. I held his hand and laid my head on his chest. Pa must have thought I was crying because he tried to look at me. I raised my head so he could see I was okay. He went back to sleep, and I laid my head down again. I could feel the warmth of his hand in mine, listened to him snoring, and I could feel and hear his heart beating. I took it all in, and it is something I will treasure for the rest of my life. I stood staring at him for a long time, just admiring how wonderful and strong he is, taking in every bit of him.

Pa was only awake for very short moments in the days after that. In between, he gave us a few smiles. He was struggling to breathe, and so I went to tell the nurse. When I looked back, I saw that Hamish was standing with him, and Pa had his hand on the back of Hamish's head, playing with his hair and stroking the back of his head. These moments, while they may not seem very much, meant the world to me. I got to speak with the doctor, and he said that it would probably only be a matter of hours or days that Pa had left.

On Sunday 14th August, all the family went into the hospital to give Pa a Fathers' Day, all of us knowing that he wasn't going to be around come September. We each wrote him a card and read it to him one at a time. Pa spent a lot of time looking behind us, or up towards the ceiling as if someone was there with us. He had been doing it the last few days every now and then but that day he was doing it a lot. I asked him a few times who he was looking at and told him that I knew someone was there, and he simply smiled at me. I had an overwhelming feeling of peace and happiness while I was there, and it actually took my breath away.

The next few days were spent in and out of the hospital, visiting Pa as much as I could. I began to notice that Pa's hand squeezes became less and less strong as time went on, and it was obvious that he was becoming much weaker. It was Thursday, and it had now been thirteen days since he had suffered the stroke. Around ten o'clock that night, after having spent all day with him, something was telling me to go home, so I did.

I was woken up by my phone ringing, and it was Mum. "He's asleep now," she said quietly, and I could hear her crying. I felt relief, as I knew that Pa was no longer in pain or struggling, but it broke my heart all the same. Mum said he went peacefully, after taking two very quiet last breaths. Nan was holding his hand. Pa passed away at 1:22 am on 19th August 2011, and I had officially lost the most amazing man I will ever know.

Pa's funeral was beautiful. My brother, my mum and I each gave a eulogy. While I was standing up there, pouring my heart out in front of all who loved Pa, I felt heartbroken, but I also felt proud. Proud to have had him as my grandfather and someone who I had looked up to throughout my life. I also felt extremely lucky that my son was blessed with knowing him. While Pa's death was a painful experience, he also gave me the strength to recognise that during his last days, he had given me a wonderful gift; he had brought my mum and I back together.

All of the good memories that Mum and I had made over my life started slowly coming back after that. Somehow I had blocked a lot of them out of my mind, and I realised I had only been focusing on the negatives all that time. I started to remember all the wonderful moments I had with Mum, like her driving all over the state to take me to dance competitions and giving me advice and so much support when Hamish was a baby and I was a Mum for the first time. Although Mum had made some mistakes, the outcome of the choices she made were just part of the lessons I had learned and the experiences that made me the person I am today. In my heart, I finally forgave her.

In late 2012, Dave I were married in Las Vegas. It was the perfect setting because neither of us wanted a big wedding, and for me, I just wanted to be able to call him my husband. What was important to me was being able to declare my love for Dave and not worry about anyone else. It was a wonderful day, and it was stress-free, which is what we both needed after the few years we'd had.

Shortly after we returned from our trip, we found out that I was pregnant. Telling Hamish was my favourite part of finding out, as he had been telling us for so long that he longed for a baby brother or sister, and Dave and I were over the moon. We went for our dating scan where I was excited for Dave to be able to see and hear our baby's heartbeat for the very first time, when our elation turned to anxiety. We were told that the pregnancy was suspected to be ectopic but that there was still a possibility the baby was okay. The next week was spent in and out of the hospital as I was given test after test but with no definitive answer. Eventually after nearly two weeks, the doctor sat Dave and I down to tell us that we had lost our baby. I felt like my heart had been ripped out. I thought it was unfair and wondered if I had done something wrong. Why didn't we get to keep our baby?

I very quickly realised just how much support I had around me, and although I struggled with understanding the whole thing, talking about it really helped me. The hardest part was telling Hamish, and we remained positive when he told us he thought it was his "only chance at getting a brother or sister." Both Dave and Hamish were amazing support, and I realised how much my baby boy had grown up every time he came up and hugged me, just saying, "It's OK Mum, I know you're upset about the baby," when I was feeling down.

The last couple of years of my life have been challenging, but they have also been a period of reflection and finding myself. I am beginning to understand that I needn't be afraid to just be myself, and I have learnt that it helps to let out my tears every so often. There have been many people that have come and gone in my life, but I have also discovered that some people come into your life for a short while, occasionally just to teach you a lesson. It took me a long time to recognise this but I'm now able to fully appreciate the people in my life that matter, and to not waste time fretting over those that don't bring positivity into my life.

I have been able to let go of a lot of negativity from my life and have learnt that not all problems can be fixed—especially if they aren't your own. I am a naturally empathetic person, but while I can feel compassion for people, I am learning to remove myself from their emotions. Someone very wise told me something that has stuck with me and helps me every day: While I am sympathetic to some people's problems, I do not own them.

I believe that with tragedy and heartbreak, comes strength. Although initially this may sound far from appealing, I am certain that my experiences have shaped me and allowed me to develop traits that I may not have had if I had not endured them. I am a strong believer that all things happen for a reason and that all experiences, good and bad, help us stay on the path that we were meant to travel.

About Christie Lyons

Hello I am Christie Lyons. I am in my early thirties and live with my husband and son in the outer suburbs of Melbourne. I am an emotional person, and have a great love of children. For the past three years I have been devoted to my career as a centre director of a not for profit childcare and kindergarten.

I enjoy travelling and would love to see more of the world. I take pleasure in experiencing different cultures and discovering places that have a lot of history. Whenever I get the chance, I love to read, and I spend a lot of time reading about spiritual theories, as well as exploring my own spirituality.

I began writing creatively as a child, but for some reason my passion became lost for a while. In early

2013, after the loss of a pregnancy, writing found its way back into my life with the help of adoptamum.com and I found that the words flowed easily. Christie now writes articles for adoptamum.com and has kindly shared some of her work in our 'Collection of Articles' section.

Christie does not stop at writing and nurturing the young through her childcare career, she is also a very gifted angel card reader at
www.soulsistashealing.com

Full Circle

By Karen Mc Dermott

There was a period in my life, not so long ago, when I had become a slave to expectation. Not any expectation that was imposed upon me but an expectation that I had imposed onto myself to meet the needs of others, and I was sacrificing too much of myself in the process. I felt like I was living my life for everyone else and not myself. I was playing follow the leader, whereas I was used to being my own leader. I did not realise that it didn't have to be this way. To allow myself something would not result in me losing it all; in fact in hindsight, it would enhance my experience of life, and because I was happier those around me would reap the benefits also. I needed to find the 'me' that I had lost a time back. I needed to keep moving forward and get back to the happy vibrant glowing me that I once was. I needed to turn full circle.

My Childhood

I was the first born into my family. I was prayed for because my parents had lost their first pregnancy, and as they were not long married when this happened, they felt the loss terribly. My father glows when he recounts to me how I was the spitting image of him when I was born. My mother laughs that I was a full month overdue; she was lying in the hospital for weeks, and every attempt to induce labour was not successful. When I finally decided to make an appearance into the world, I had outgrown some of my skin, namely on my bottom, and my parents were not allowed to take me home with them when it was time to leave the hospital a week later. Things were done a lot slower those days in Ireland. Mum has often recalled to me the excitement of getting up one morning and dashing to the phone box to phone the hospital and see how I was when she was given the news that the doctor had cleared me to go home. As we had no family car, mum recalls that she ran down to the main road and hitch-hiked a lift to the big town and ordered a taxi to take me and her home. When my father arrived home on his lunch break from the local factory, mum had me propped up on the sofa and never said a word until he saw me sitting there like a 'mini me'. Now family life could begin.

I have always felt lucky to have been given the parents that I have. I have always had a close connection with my dad; it is an unspoken natural bond that I treasure dearly, and looking back it has always given me a secure foundation on which to grow. But it is my mum who raised us all; she has always encouraged me to live my dreams and been a support through the good times and the bad. She is one of those mums that you can call on anytime, no judgements and no expectations.

My parents came from different situations; they were raised on the same street yet experienced life so differently. My father was cared for by his grandparents when he was young. My mother was number six in a household of twelve children. When my mum and dad got together and started a family, it is understandable that they wanted to create a loving home and a secure loving family bond so that their children could flourish out into the world with the stability and support of loving parents.

Looking back on my young childhood, I know that I was very fortunate to have been given my parents and I never take that for granted. I have and still do learn so much from them. Christmases and Birthdays have always been very special and my mum always makes a lot of effort no matter what else is going on at the time. I believe in the magic of life because of my mum's efforts.

I always felt very much loved; this feeling of unconditional love has stayed with me and made me feel safe and indestructible. I was the first born of six, three girls and then three boys. Family was always everything to me; we all have always had a very strong bond, and I have always felt a huge loyalty to my family. I never imagined living one day of my life without contact let alone living the other side of the globe with the prospect of never seeing them again; however, life sometimes has a strange way of directing us in alternative directions than what we expect, and I have learned to not resist unexpected changes, as they often have a positive outcome.

A big change for me, when I was young, was when we moved from the Republic of Ireland to the North of Ireland. Even though we only geographically shifted one and a half miles 'out the road', it was a major change in lifestyle and thinking. We were leaving the close-knit community of town life to embrace a more isolated existence in the countryside. It is all part of my journey to where I am now and my parents were fulfilling a dream to build a house on a hill and I always remember feeling so proud of that.

Looking back on my childhood, now that I am a mum myself, I know that we all are still learning about life even when we become parents and that as children we just expect our parents to be perfectly grounded when in actual fact they are still human and can make mistakes also. I consider myself fortunate because my parents did, and still do, everything with the right intention and for our family and through them I have learned so much about life. When you have that kind of support you never feel alone.

When I was sixteen I chose not to stay at school and I applied for a job in a factory, which I got. It felt good to earn my own money. I then moved back to a job in my home town. It felt perfect, something shifted in me when that happened; it was as if I had come home as if I belonged again. I felt more grounded and had a desire to set some foundations to my life. I was more settled and started going out with someone who I had known since my early school years. I felt grown up; I began wanting things like a home, a commitment, and a baby, and that is how it happened.

When, at eighteen, I discovered that I was pregnant it was quite a shock. My father was disappointed, which was to be expected, but my mother, she was such a great support and assured me that everything would be ok, a real rock when I needed it most. I know that without that support my pregnancy would have been a more negative experience.

Over the next year I grew up very quickly. I loved being a mum so much, my son was my life. I worked hard and was focused on moving forward, but unfortunately my partner did not grow up at the same speed I did and we drifted apart.

I was now a 20-year-old single mum, but with the support of my wonderful mum, I was able to keep working and moving forward. I had a blip where I had a distracting relationship with my supervisor who was ten years my senior, but that didn't evolve as I had hoped and we went our separate ways; he went to America, I stayed in the factory and was offered his supervisory position. Financially things were improving, and I was enjoying the unexpected new-found responsibility in my work. I decided to give it another go with my son's dad. I really made an effort, but I was soon to discover that we were still not compatible; however,

I felt guilty and so stayed in the relationship longer than I should of. I was still only a young 23 at this stage. I finally found the courage to move forward and so I ended the relationship, and he moved to America (this was becoming a trend).

I changed my approach to life after that, and things became more positive for me again. I was enjoying being a single mum, and I had good friends around me and a wonderful relationship with my sister also. I left my supervisory job, and I found a part time job and went back to college. Money was tight, but money wasn't everything.

I was astounded to learn that I loved learning; I had never felt this way about knowledge before. It was as if I had caught a learning bug, and I needed to absorb all of the information I could find. I did a Foundation course and discovered that I loved English and media. The course was two years long and was not easy, but I juggled everything so well. I had balance, and my heart was singing.

When I was 25 I met someone; I didn't feel as though there was any room in my life for a relationship, but I decided after a while to give it a go with this person as he seemed keen and, although he was not my usual type as he had a bad-boy image, I connected with something in him. I realise now that it was his intention.

It was as if something shifted to allow this relationship to happen as my son's dad was back from America and he was keen to see him at the weekends. As my new partner worked away during the week, weekends were the only time we could get time together, and so I gave it a go. It soon became serious, and within six months I had moved out of my lovely little house and began setting up home with him and my son. I was to work harder to keep this all together. I had two jobs, I was finishing my course, and, as I did not want to change my son from his school, I ensured that I did all that I could to keep him there.

Then I met a crossroads. I was accepted into university but that meant shifting my whole life to the top of Ireland, and it didn't feel like the right time to do that. At the same time, an opening came up in administration that I was really interested in doing. I chose the job and to study humanities part time and I was offered another part-time job with the local college tutoring in out-centres. Everything I was asking for from life was happening, but I was juggling so much—college, two jobs, parenthood, a new relationship and commuting long distances. Something had to give, and when I lost my driving license for a year because of drunk driving, I was soon to realise that it was the commuting that was going to go. It was a tough year, but I managed to keep my jobs, complete my course, be there for my son and have a relationship. Lesson learned!

I was then offered a scholarship to a year-long, once-a-month intensive drama course; I had the opportunity to visit various locations all around Ireland, the only problem being that it was at weekends. Was I going to stretch things too far again? I chose to accept the scholarship, and although it was tough, I adjusted for that year. I discovered so many things about myself during the course as many of the things we explored directly connected with my inner self, this was something I would often shy away from facing. I didn't know if the outer me was really expressing what the inner me felt. My confidence was an issue on top of the list in addition to some incidents of intimidation throughout my life that had affected me deeply— one from my English teacher and one from a work mate who used to pick on me to make me blush really badly. It was intense, but it had to be, as we were being taught to go out there and help others overcome their social and personal problems through drama therapy. At the end of the course, we put on a production. I was astonished to discover that I could remember a script; I have never had the best memory. I loved this experience! Because of the qualification I got from the course I was offered a position through the local college teaching drama to adults with special needs. I loved this job so much and found it was very natural for me to give in this way to others. It was hard work but so rewarding.

The play we staged at the end of my course 'Lipstick Powder and Politics' was chosen to tour, I was so excited, but what I didn't know is that I was actually pregnant at the time and so I had to pull out. That was ok though because my partner and I were so excited and had been trying for a baby for some time and it hadn't been happening and with my new job I knew that it was a sign to focus on what I had already achieved.

We had recently bought a block of land with an old house on it, and we decided to do it up and make it liveable until we built a new house on the block.

The U-turn

There was something about that house. I loved the quaintness of it, but things began going downhill when we moved there. It was as if life had done a u-turn and was steadily going downhill. The only good thing that happened over the next two years was the healthy birth of our son. I felt like I was being made pay for anything I did wrong in my life. It was a tough time, and after an incident occurred that sunk me low enough to suffer post-traumatic stress, we decided to embark on setting up a whole new life for ourselves in Australia. Luckily, I knew what was wrong with me, as I had been working in a Mental Health setting for a number of years, and I allowed myself to be guided through my recovery by listening to my inner spirit. I slowed my life way down, and for the next year I took each moment as it came and dealt with life accordingly. I was getting stronger each day.

We began building the new house and, in the back of our minds, hoped to get a residency visa to Australia, but if we didn't then at least we would have a new family home. I was just going along with things during this time, and when I discovered I was expecting, it was light—a positive light—shining into our lives again. I had not considered having another child but it seemed so right and I felt a glow again. This was to be a short-lived elation as I was to miscarry a few weeks later. I was distraught, I couldn't stop crying. I wanted that baby so much; it was going to make everything better again. I prayed so hard every single night that I would be filled again as I felt so empty. I couldn't understand why this happened to me. It was during this time my partner, who was my rock, and I also received great support from my parents which brought us all closer again. But what I didn't realise then is that this harrowing time in my life was to shift me back onto my right path. It was the wakeup call that I had needed. Everything started to fall into place. My relationship was back on track, and my partner proposed. This was in December, and we booked the wedding for May. It felt so right. I saw how strong my partner was when I really needed him, and it made me feel so protected, which I really needed at the time.

Choosing to get married was a really big deal for me as I had always said that I was never going to get married and contentment was my worst enemy, but now I had changed my thinking on this and the actions were following. Contentment was what I craved and getting married felt like the next step for me.

Then it all came together

It was as if the angel of all good things came knocking on our door. I discovered that my prayers had been answered and I was expecting again. We then received notification that we had been granted full residency status for Australia. This was going to be a busy year! What a transition. It was as if we had jumped off the treadmill of life that made me feel as if I was going nowhere, just getting slower and slower; however, I now realise that this was my preparation time, and my wait was now over. I was now ready to run the gauntlet of life again.

Moving to Australia was something I know that I was destined to do. I was thirty-one when we moved. It has given me the space that I so desperately needed to grow within myself. I now know what people mean when they say that they 'found themselves'; I truly did. I don't know if I needed to move to the other side of the world to do this but I did need space in which to deal with all of the raw emotions that come with evolving this way.

A few weeks after we arrived in Australia, I had my third child, and my creativity blossomed. I was so connected to parenthood, and I began writing and illustrating children's books. I was making myself happy and my children happy. In one year, I wrote and illustrated about thirty books for my children.

I then fell pregnant again for my fourth child. I know that being pregnant has allowed me to be emotional. I have given myself permission to be vulnerable; many see this as a weakness, I now class it as strength.

I went through a rough patch were, through my thoughts and dreams, I relived situations of my past. Even years later, these situations needed me to feel the suppressed emotions that I had hidden deep down inside me. I have embraced forgiveness—forgiveness of myself as well as others—and this has freed me from the shackles of the past to allow me to move forward.

I realised then that life is learning and everything that we encounter in our lifetime is in the best interest in the advancement of our spirit and it is individual to us. Whether someone is a positive or a negative influence in my life, I still learn from them. Whether it is momentary or for a time, I have learned something from each interaction I have had, and it is important to deal with the emotions that surface because that helps us to grow as a person.

This cleansed me, my heart opened up, and I was ready to embrace life again. I had allowed myself to connect with my inner guide, and all of a sudden I understood things. I was thinking for myself again, whereas I hadn't wanted that responsibility for some time because of the consequences that may arise from my choices. Fear was limiting me from embracing life fully. I chose to honour the fear that I felt and to follow my heart by replacing it with love.

Discovering my inner writer!

My beautiful friend, Donna, introduced me to her new website, and it was called Adopt a Mum. I decided to join, and here I was introduced to new and exciting things. I began writing in the groups and got such wonderful responses that I began writing longer pieces. It wasn't long before I was writing weekly articles about things I was discovering about my spiritual journey. Writing was giving me a way to release so much from inside. I couldn't stop. I was receiving signs from all around, and the serendipity of the signs that were happening amazed me. I realised that I had become more aware of life on a different level. I was living on a different frequency and attracting things more easily because of that.

It was when my fourth child was four weeks old that I embarked on the mission to write a book. At first I did not have a clue what I was going to write about; I had never planned or written a story before, so I wasn't 100% sure what I needed to do. All I knew is that it felt so right and everything was aligned for me to achieve it. The chain of serendipitous events happened like this: I was first introduced to the possibility of writing 50000 words by my beautiful friend when she told me that she had sat down and written 50000 words about her life. This flipped the switch of possibility on, and I was so inspired by this possibility. Then, in my inbox came a message from an annual challenge which invited writers to write 50000 words in a month by meeting a daily target of 1667 words. Again, I just knew that it was right for me. But what was I going to write about?

I then had a surreal experience when one day I was watching *'The View'* and there was a celebrity couple on who had suffered a miscarriage; I felt their pain. Whoopi Goldberg stopped the show to say to them that she tells her girlfriends that when someone miscarries it is a Visitor that has come to prepare them for receiving the true gift because maybe they weren't on the right path or ready. This resonated with me beyond belief, I was uplifted, and in that instant I had been gifted with the spiritual understanding of why I had experienced a miscarriage. I felt compelled to share this with others to help them. Within a few days I began the writing challenge, and one month later *The Visitor ~ a magical understanding of uncertainty* was finished.

I know that my writing may conjure up unwanted feelings in some people; however, I do write with the truest of intention, which is to help others heal and see an alternative perspective— some people are ready and some people are not, and that is fine.

I put it out there into the universe that I really wanted to have this book published and it was. The gorgeous person who introduced me to the possibility of actually writing a book was also the person who made the opportunity available for me to publish my book. This lady has definitely had a profoundly positive impact on my life as a friend and someone who believes in me so much. I will always be truly grateful to her for being such a positive in my life.

As my book was being published I learned so much about the whole process of book publishing. So when the opportunity found me early 2012 to set up *Inner Light Publishing*, I listened to my heart and I knew it was the right thing to do. Since then it has grown at a steady and magical pace. Everything we needed to know came to us just as we needed to know it. Our vision is clear: we want to share as many stories with others as we can and this we will do. It also turned out that we are helping authors and community groups self-publish their books economically and positively. When we follow our hearts, things come together effortlessly.

I have had my work published on adoptamum.com, in publications all over the world as well as in a monthly magazine called *Universal Mind*, and I have even had the opportunity to be published on mamamia.com. I have since written and published the next book in *The Enlightenment Series* called *The Wish Giver*, and I am soon to finish *The Memory Taker*.

The lessons I have learned so far is that spiritually we are on this earth to grow. We all work towards the same goal of enlightenment within, some of us acknowledge it and have an easier ride and others don't. I have learned to forgive everyone and everything; this is for my greater good. I endeavour to ensure that everything I do is executed with the truest of intention. I have also realised that I cannot be responsible for how others react to me but I can be responsible for how I react to others.

I have embraced the universal *Law of Attraction* in a spiritual way, and I know that by releasing positive, loving energy out into the world I am doing my bit to attract it back to me. I choose not to feel fear; I choose to live in the power that I have been gifted with, and I choose to live my best life. To further enhance my knowledge on the power of attraction, I have completed Advanced Law of Attraction training, and I am now a certified practitioner.

I have now rotated full circle and live my life, once again, with passion and love, and this makes my heart sing!

I truly do live **MY** dream! Being a mum to five wonderful children and being able to write and help others is what I am destined to do, it feels so right and I am grateful to have the opportunity to feel so fulfilled, there are many people who never find what it is that makes their heart sing and I have so much that makes mine beat a harmonious tune every day.

I know that I may have challenges to face in my lifetime, but now I can face them with a renewed understanding of life. I have been fortunate to come to this understanding at a young age, and it will help me give the best of myself to others and that is what

I endeavour to do. I am living the perfect life for me. I have created it for myself, and I am grateful for it every day. I encourage everyone to keep a little for yourself—do something that makes your heart sing!

I have come *Full Circle* as I now live my life with passion and love again. My secret recipe to being happy is to embark on life with the right intention, be willing to adjust your perspective when need be, be aware of the bigger picture of what is going on around you, and listen to your inner guide; you will know when things are right for you and waste less time steering off your true path. Finally, love yourself; you are your own best friend.

I do hope that you have enjoyed reading my journey thus far; I know that I have still so much to experience from life but this I do with a greater sense of awareness and an overwhelming appreciation to my family and loved ones who show me so much support even when I falter.

I have added a piece I wrote about my journey, physically and emotionally, to Australia, I hope that from my journey you may gain some insight.

/ Journey to Inner Light

A New Life

By Karen Mc Dermott

Just about to board the plane; I am heading down under. What should I be feeling? What do I feel? I don't know—maybe numbness if I had to pick something, everything just seems so surreal. Maybe this is how my body and mind deal with dramas now, just to get on with the task in hand and deal with the impact later. Or more likely, I have just gone into auto pilot; I am 35 weeks pregnant after all, and the full impact of this dramatic life-change could hit anytime, and I may not make it to Australia, but I must remember it is not just me to consider there are my two young sons and my husband too.

We are starting a new life together as a complete family unit. This is what I really want for us, but why do I not feel really excited? Where are the butterflies that should be doing somersaults in my tummy with anticipation? Maybe what I am sacrificing to fulfil my dream is so much that it all balances itself out to a feeling of nothing. How sad that thought is; however, it is not going to change anything thinking like that. I have made the decision to change things in my life, and my goodness how I have changed things. I can only hope and pray that it all turns out well, and that I had made the right decision two years ago in the depths of anxiety. Have I been stubborn and stupid, or am I adventurous and wise?

The last few years have been torturous to my soul. The independent go-getter got a psychological battering and didn't feel safe in her own skin anymore. I will be honest and say that I felt totally betrayed by each and every one in my family when they reacted the way they did when my brother went crazy in my home. The effects of post-traumatic stress are shocking, it shakes you from the core, and it eluded a great darkness inside of me that caused me to close the shutters to the outside world. I started to live day by day, trying to do the best for my partner and children. I left my job, which I loved, and my home felt different as regular flash backs occurred frequently.

I felt no reason to stay somewhere that made me and my family unhappy. There was no longer anything holding me back from our dream of moving to Australia, so we applied for our visas. When I let everyone know our plans, the disbelief that they all had was not unexpected. They thought that I wouldn't actually see it through and that I was just running away from everything, but they also knew that once I had my mind set on something I never give up until I have succeeded. But then again, they thought that side of me was not around anymore.

For a full year after, our luck was shocking; not only was I trying to keep strong for my family but also everything we did or touched went wrong. I remember the cars, how much bad luck did we have with cars over that time—even the car Dad lent me blew a radiator within a week. It couldn't just be maintenance issues, there had to be bad luck in it, too. We bought a sporty car and paid dearly to make it the way we wanted, and then its engine seized the day I picked it up from the garage. What are the chances of that? Mind you, if that had of been all, I could have dealt with that as they were just material things.

The time I thought that our luck had changed was when I discovered that I was pregnant; there seemed to be light gleaming from the end of the tunnel, and oh how I wanted it so much. I couldn't wait to tell everyone, and then to discover that little sis was expecting too, for the same time, was fantastic. I finally felt happiness again, and I was making plans in my head. The morning I discovered the blood was indescribable. "Why me?" is all that I could think. I rested in bed in a desperate attempt to save the pregnancy, but one week later it disappeared. I know exactly when it happened as I lay there analysing every movement in my uterus. I was distraught, and my partner was such a rock for me in my vulnerable state even though he was feeling the loss too. He had done so much over the last week to make things easier. I remember just lying at nights, feeling empty, praying to be full again. I knew that the pain would not go away until I filled that void, the feeling was uncontrollable. If anything good was to come out of the whole experience it was that it made me feel protected and so loved by my strong partner, and it brought us so close together again. That was when we decided to get married. When I look back now, it was as if the diamond dazzler that he bought me changed my life. I know now that it was at that point that our luck changed.

We booked the wedding for May, and in February we discovered that I was expecting again, everything was changing for the better. Of course, initially the fear of possibly losing another pregnancy hit me, but I took it easy. Then there was the wedding to organise in just a few months. It wasn't ideal to be slowing down, but so what; the main thing was that things seemed to be working out for a change, and all of the rest would fall into place.

I remember the day I went to pick up our rings. It was the brightest, sunniest day of the year so far. I had a glow around me and a smile on my face again; no one or nothing was going to drag me down. I was at the counter paying for the rings when my phone rang. It was the visa application centre, and the Australian migration department had granted our visas. We could now become full residents of Australia if we wanted. "Oh my goodness what a year, what a turn of luck.

We had to enter Australia before December. Our baby was due in October and we had no visa for her, so we had no choice but to go soon. In one year: get married, finish building a house, migrate to the other side of the world and have a baby. These are things people do over their lifetime, not all in one year. It has to be done though; "Everything happens for a reason" is what I kept telling myself and others. I am just going to enjoy these good times and not take anything for granted ever again.

The wedding was great, low key and we did what we wanted, which was sweet and intimate and enjoyed by all. The flowers were lilies, and the man from the flower shop lent us tall vases to put them in. The scene of me and my sisters running into the chapel a few days after the wedding to retrieve the vases still sticks with me to this day. The chapel is close to my heart, as it was where my mum and dad got married; my granny always attended, and I felt her spirit with me there; my children were christened; and the priest was non-judgemental and fun. In fact, he had a motorbike and hung out with all walks of life, and he worked hard to get the young people back to mass.

The finishing of the house was not all plain sailing. My new hubby was doing most of the work himself, and time was quickly going in. We still had not got our tickets booked for Australia as money was tight and what we had we needed to finish the house. Everything was up in the air, it was now July and I did not know where I was going or what our plans were going to be for the next six months. I was getting bigger and bigger every day, and my pregnancy was a bit tough, but we stayed focused on getting things ready for leaving even though we had no flights booked.

Then we did it, we gathered the money to get our tickets and booked them for the first of

September—the first day of spring in Australia and the first day of autumn in Ireland. Those next few weeks were surreal to say the least. So much to organise but "where there is a will there is always a way." It rained a lot during that time. I remember a lot of darkness in the weather and a lot of disbelief that I was actually going. I was running from pillar to post trying to spend time with my family, get ready for leaving and prepare finances. Over the years, we had accumulated a lot of things, which we put into the new garage, and told our families to take what they liked. We got the new house completed just in time, which was a huge challenge in itself. I don't know how my hubby did it all himself but he did. I wasn't much help waddling around.

Families from both sides organised some leaving parties, which was so nice of everyone. It is good to have those memories to take with us and nice to leave with positive thoughts even if they were filled with a lot of emotion. However, I do remember my sister saying to me that it was as if I was dying and preparations were being made accordingly as pictures of me were being hung up all over the family home.

The morning came, and it was time to go. The last week had been so exhausting mentally and physically as we got prepared for our departure. We were so close to going nowhere as our finances had fallen through a few days prior. We stuck with it and didn't give up, and it has paid off. If it is worth having it is worth fighting for, and it makes you appreciate it all the more. I went up to my family home where everyone had gathered to say goodbye. All was very strange, and I was again very numb to emotion. There was the usual banter that happens when all of the family gathers, which was good as it kept everything going. My parents and sister had been to a wedding the night before, and to my horror my father was still quite under the influence, and as he was to chauffeur us to the airport, it was a bit of a problem. This was strange as my father was never a real drinker at all; however, my brother-in-law came to the rescue and offered to drive us. We said our last goodbyes, and I tried my best to hold back the tears. With a big lump in my throat, we drove away. I dropped my son off at his father's house to say goodbye to his grandparents and other relations, and his dad was following us to the airport so that he could see him off.

The journey to the airport was not an easy one. We were squashed in the back of a car; my two year old was impatient, my tipsy father was in the passenger seat not feeling very well, and he did not smell very well either, come to think of it, which did not help me in my situation. Then there were all of the detours because of road works, and we got lost. It wasn't really going to plan, but we had left in good time. When we finally got to the airport, I said a quick goodbye and fled as I felt tears coming. When inside the terminal, there was another problem. Where was my eldest son? I had thoughts of his father abducting and all sorts of things. But by the skin of his teeth, he arrived so we went and checked in at the desk.

Just as we were getting ready to enter the terminal, my phone rang. It was my in-laws; they had come to surprise us at the airport. "Oh no, more tears" is what I thought initially, as I knew I was on the verge of letting all of mine flow out. We said more goodbyes and got through to the gate where—*phew*—we could now breathe. To say I was on an emotional rollercoaster would be an understatement, and I still had numerous hours of flying and no sleeping to face. I do hope that it has all been worth it. It is now time for us to depart from our previous life to set up another on the other side of the world. My journey to departures has now ended, and a new chapter of my life has just begun.

About Karen Mc Dermott

Karen Mc Dermott began her writing journey at adoptamum.com. in 2010. Filled to the brim with creativeness after having her 4th child she began writing short pieces of interest, this soon grew into featured articles and then her first novel *The Visitor* was born through the belief and support she received from adoptamum.com. Karen knows that it is because she was given the opportunity to discover her natural writing ability through the freedom of exploration that she has successfully incorporated writing into her life.

Consistently building upon her desire to write, learn and help others she has now published her second novel *The Wish Giver* and her third, *The Memory Taker* is due for release in 2013.

With her fifth child due in May 2013 and the publishing company Inner Light Publishing, that she co-founded in 2012 with the support and affiliation of adoptamum.com, her path appears to be very clearly focused on babies and books.

"I am living my dream, I am truly blessed"

Speaking publically has also been an aspect of writing that she is getting more comfortable with as she knows that through her journey others may be inspired.

A certified Law of Attraction Practitioner, Karen has truly attracted everything that she has ever dreamt of into her life and she aspires to helping others do the same.

Karen has shared some of her articles at the back of this book in the 'Collection of Articles' chapter.

Karen can be contacted on facebook Karen Mc Dermott (Weaver) or twitter #karenmcdermott4

A collection of articles

SHARED BY: ANDREW JOBLING, MARY LYNCH, KAREN MC DERMOTT AND CHRISTIE LYONS.

1. **The Angel Inside you just needs… TO BE SET FREE!** Written by Andrew Jobling
2. **You don't get what you want …You get what you expect!** Written by Andrew Jobling
3. **To launch into an amazing day …Love the morning!** Written by Andrew Jobling
4. **Acceptance** Written by Mary Lynch
5. **Misdiagnosis ~ The story of a "cute" schizophrenic** Written by Mary Lynch
6. **I want to know what love is** Written by Mary Lynch
7. **Personal evolution : To become a butterfly?** Written by Karen Mc Dermott
8. **The answer is Love** Written by Karen Mc Dermott
9. **Spirituality** Written by Karen Mc Dermott
10. **Starting to Heal** Written by Christie Lyons
11. **I was there all along** Written by Christie Lyons
12. **My Jelly Bean** Written by Christie Lyons

Andrew Jobling

The Angel Inside you just needs... TO BE SET FREE!

Written by Andrew Jobling

My gorgeous wife Laura spoke of some things I didn't know this week and it really sparked an interest in me. Laura comes from a proud Italian heritage and she told me all about the famous *Statue of David* in Florence. Did you know that the statue, representing the biblical hero David, stands 5.17 metres (17 feet) tall and was carved from one single block of marble between the years of 1501 and 1504 by artist Michelangelo? Can you imagine having one massive 10 ton block of marble in front of you and, from it, creating such beauty and such detail as was the *Statue of David*? I did some research and was most inspired and excited by a couple of quotes by the artist Michelangelo. When he was asked how he made the statue he was reported to have said, *"It is easy. You just chip away the stone that doesn't look like David."* Then he made the statement that has really inspired this week's article ... *"I saw the angel in the marble and I just carved until I set him free."*

When I look at the statue I am in absolute awe. Laura has actually seen it in Florence and has stood before it ... in her words, she says it is *"overwhelmingly majestic with its own powerful energy ... like it is singing to me."* She said she stood there for 20 minutes - staring - lost in its majesty and power. Just an incredible vision of beauty, power and majesty which all started from a massive lump of marble!

That beauty, power and majesty is inside of you

You may be wondering where I am heading with all of this talk about the *Statue of David*. It must have a point, and it does ... an incredibly significant and profound one. Michelangelo spoke about the *'angel in the marble'* that just needed to be *'set free'*. The *Statue of David* is you! You are the angel in the marble – the simple question is; have you set yourself free yet?

Michelangelo stated that it is easy ... just chip away the bits that don't look like you. You know, deep down, the person that you want to be ...don't you? You want to be happy, healthy, confident, successful, significant, lean, loved and loving – anything else you can think of? Do you know that the person you want to be is already inside of you? You just need to chip away the things that are covering the real you – the things that are not you but are masking the angel that lies underneath.

I am talking about getting rid of the things that are preventing you from being the amazing person that you are – the things stopping you from seeing the beautiful, powerful and majestic winner that is the real you. And believe me ... you are amazing! So what is holding you back? What is keeping the angel stuck beneath the surface? What is preventing the real you from showing your majesty? Is it lack of belief? Is it low self esteem? Is it lack of confidence or fear of failure? Is it worrying about what other people will think? Those things are not you – they are roadblocks preventing the real you from shining through and showing what you are capable of. So ... are you ready to chisel?

Get a chisel and start chipping ...

The first step is to really believe that the angel is in you. This is the first layer of chiseling you need to begin with. So think now - and I mean right now – of things that you have already achieved in your life. Think of the things that you are proud of; the work you do, the family you have raised and/or the courses you have completed.

Think of the people you have impacted, the home you live in, the way you look or have looked and the hills you have climbed. Think of the hardest thing you have ever done ... the thing that took an incredible effort and, at times, you wanted to give up on. Think about how you kept going and you got it done! With all this achievement, how could you possibly not believe in yourself or your own power? Are you with me?

Okay, the next level of chiseling is to start to chip away at the voice in your head that is saying *'I can't'* and begin replacing it with the voice telling you that you can and you deserve the best. Start telling yourself that you can, you have and you will. Start affirming what you want by writing down and reading positive, empowering and abundance statements to yourself every day. This will take some time, consistency and discipline but the result will be setting free the angel – the powerful and amazing you - that is underneath.

When you look in the mirror do you see the beautiful and majestic *Statue of David*, or do you see a lump of rock? Either way the news is great. If you are facing a lump of marble ... look deeply and see the angel that lies underneath, then simply start carving until you set it free. You are the Michelangelo of your life!

You don't get what you want ... You get what you expect!

Written by Andrew Jobling

There are many things in my life that I wish I had. I have written down lists of dreams & goals and whilst I have achieved some of them, I certainly have not come close to achieving everything I want ... I have really only just scratched the surface of my list.

After serious thought, research and reflection about why that is, I have finally realised the answer. I don't get everything I want, but I will get everything I expect ...

The Experiment

An experiment was conducted in a San Francisco bay area school by a Dr Robert Rosenthal of Harvard University – he worked with the principal of the school. At the beginning of a school year the principal called three teachers into his office and told them, *"We have been watching you and as a result of your teaching excellence over the last three or four years we have concluded that you are consistently the best 3 teachers in the school."*

"*As a special reward to you*", he told the three teachers, "*We have identified three classes with 30 students in each class ... these are the brightest students in the school with the highest IQ's and we are going to assign them to you to teach for the entire year.*"

"*Now, we don't want to be accused of discrimination, so it is very important that you don't tell the children, in any way, that they have been selected for a screened class. Second of all we are not going to tell the parents, because we don't want to cause any difficulties there either.*" The principal continued, "*I expect you to teach exactly the same way you normally do and use exactly the same curriculum ...and I expect you to get very very good results with these students.*"

The Results

At the end of the school year these students led, not only, the school but the entire district in academic accomplishment. Calling the three teachers into his office at the end of the school year, the principal of the school said, "*Well, we have had a very good year haven't we?*" "*Yes we have,*" the teachers said, "*it was really easy ... these children were very easy to teach in fact. They were eager to learn and it was such a pleasure to teach them.*"

"*Well, maybe I had better tell you the truth,*" the principal explained. "*This has been an experiment and those 90 students were just chosen at random out of a hat. We assigned them to you at the start of the year with no idea what their IQ was at all.*" The surprised teachers said, "*That is incredible ... oh, that's right we are the best teachers in the school, aren't we? That's why!" "Maybe I should tell you the rest of the story"* the principal said, *"You three were also put into hat with all the other teachers and randomly drawn out!"*

Dr Rosenthal did this experiment in 300 schools with 900 randomly selected teachers and 27,000 randomly selected students and got identical results every single time!

The conclusions

The average teachers and students did so well because of the law of positive expectancy. This law states that you achieve what you expect to achieve and what others expect you to achieve. Since the principal expected a lot, so did the teachers and sensing the teachers expected a lot, the students did too.

To achieve more you have to expect more for and from yourself. To get more from people you know, work with and care about expect more from them. But be very careful because the opposite is also true - so make sure you get into the habit of expecting the best.

The application

This is great news for you only if you can apply it into your life – TODAY! I am going to challenge you right now … think about something you wish you could have, be or do but you are not expecting it to happen. Is it losing weight, getting that promotion, asking that girl/boy out, getting selected for the team or whatever it may be? Just because I said so (and I know!), I want you to believe that you can achieve it. I also want you to expect, deep in your heart, as I expect from you (and I know!), that you will get the result. Visualise it, feel it, own it and expect it and understand that in life ... we don't get what we want, we don't get what we deserve, we always get what we expect ... every single time.

To launch into an amazing day ... Love the morning!

Written by Andrew Jobling

Are you a morning person? Do you love it when our eyes open and do you jump out of bed in anticipation of a great day? Or, are you AM challenged and cranky ... like a grizzly bear? I am a reformed grizzly bear and have gone from a diehard *'not a morning person'* to someone who now sees the morning as the time when we can set up an amazing day ... or not!

Many years ago I began a career as a personal trainer. I loved that career when I started and I loved it for many years - and lucky I did because I had to get up at 5am everyday! I did not consider myself a 'morning person' ... I know, I know I picked a bad career to be 'not a morning person'! Over time getting up early became a habit but I still considered myself 'not a morning person' and I hated it when the alarm went off.

What are you telling yourself?

I would tell myself day after day that I am not a morning person and would wake up anxious every day. I would worry that I hadn't had enough sleep and that I wouldn't have enough energy to get through the day. I would think to myself, *'I don't want to get up'* and *'if only I could have a bit more sleep'*. I would focus on the things I hadn't done and should be doing and as the alarm went off and my day was about to begin I would have this churning and anxiety in my body. As a result I was often cranky and funnily enough, many times, things didn't go the way I wanted them to go.

I realised that if I persist in telling myself I am not a morning person, then that is what I will continue to be. I would keep feeling the same way every morning and continue to get the same results day after day, week after week, year after year.

Let's face it, there is no way you can be cranky, tired, unenthusiastic and anxious in the morning and expect anything amazing to happen that day. What we experience and what we do & achieve on a daily basis is a direct reflection of our attitude. That attitude is a choice and a decision we make the second we wake up and will determine the direction of our day and … ultimately our life.

Create a morning plan that sets you up for success

So, I needed to change my morning routine. I needed to eliminate thinking about the things I didn't like, didn't want, that caused me stress &

anxiety and replace them with focusing on what I want. It sounds easy enough, but it took some time and discipline and as a result my life has changed immeasurably for the better. I love the morning and I love how it sets up my day for success ... every day. What could be better than that? Are you interested to know what I do?

The first thing I did was change my attitude towards the morning. I started to tell myself that *'I am a morning person.'* I started to see the birth of each new day as an opportunity to take another step forward and move toward the life I have always wanted.

Consequently I was keen to get out of bed and get started on my vision. I slowly developed a morning routine which I now follow religiously every day.

When I started trying to develop a positive morning routine, I didn't think I had the time, as I was often rushing in the morning because I got up too late. So my morning routine started with five minutes ... over time I developed it to about an hour. My advice for you is to start gradually and build up - trust me when I say, this morning routine will change your life forever.

This is my exact routine:

1. Metabolism and energy - I get up and straight away have a small amount of watermelon to kick start my metabolism and my spark my energy levels.

2. Affirmations - I go into the bathroom and look at myself in the mirror and read positive statements of what I want out aloud to myself three times.
3. Exercise – I do 20-30 minutes of exercise every day and I feel great after it.
4. Meditate – I simply do 5-10 minutes of sitting quietly, eyes closed and focusing only on my breathing ... to quieten my mind.
5. Morning Pages – I write three pages of stuff – whatever comes into my mind and whatever I want to get out of my head and onto paper – this is an incredibly cleansing process and helps to unload any stresses I have. As soon as I have finished these pages I tear them up and throw them away.
6. Write out my goals – I write out 10 goals I have, ranging over one week to 10 years – to get me focused on what I want.
7. Write the things that 'take my breath away' – I write out the amazing things I dream about and am working on that will 'take my breath away'. As I am writing these things I am visualising them happening – I smile inside.
8. Breakfast – I eat a healthy, natural and life giving breakfast.
9. Have a great day – I feel incredibly cleansed and focused and ready to get started on what I have to do to make all the amazing things I have visualized and written about come true.

Your challenge this week, should you choose to accept is to take the first step towards setting up your own morning routine. This routine could quite possibly be the most important thing you can do for your life, so don't confuse it for or sacrifice it with urgent things. Prioritise it, focus on it, make it a daily habit and watch your life change for the better forever.

To view more of Andrew's articles visit

www.andrewjobling.com.au/free-stuff/download-articles

Mary Lynch

Acceptance

Written by Mary Lynch

When I met her she was in her late seventies. Not a handsome woman but with a beauty that came from the soul. She walked with a confidence that was delightful to be around. Tall, elegant and peaceful. I was fascinated. What was it she had found that had made her so? So content, so loving, so kind, and so serene.

This lady had an abundance of charm and grace such that you wanted to be around. She had little to say but I needed to know more. This was the woman I wanted to be, no advertising company could portray her glow, her beauty, her faith.

'Do you have children?' I asked, as it is something every parent can relate to. I wanted to open up a conversation.

'Had,' she replied quietly.

What does that mean, my mind enquired, but I did not make it vocal?

Did she put them up for adoption, were they taken from her…..? Were they dead? She did not give any more information. I dared not ask.

She stayed a few days and every time I was in her company I didn't want to leave. The glow around her would warm the coldest being. She must be an angel I thought.

One evening when we were alone I found the courage to ask.

'What happened to you children?' She looked at me with a smile. A smile that I had seen so often in the west, a smile that said plainly, without a syllable being uttered, 'Why are you northerners so direct?'

Some people liked this trait, others were offended by it, but I had learned to use it with softness so that no offence could be taken.

'It's a long story,' she said.

I did not reply but sat back to hear it.

Her faced glowed as she started.

'I met him when I was a teenager. They say there is no such thing as love at first sight but I loved him from that moment. We clicked as they say today and from the beginning we were rarely apart. He was local. I was a blow in but his parents accepted me as if I was one of their own. They were farmers and being the eldest in the family he was to take it over. The romance bloomed over the years and we were married young. We lived with his parents for a while but then built our own house. He was always busy on the farm and I was busy with the children and my parents who came to live with us when they got older. I loved what I was doing. I loved taking care of everyone. I worked to make everyone comfortable. Everyone said that I worked too hard but it was not work to me. It was love. A labour of love. What more could any woman ask for. Taking care of the ones she loved. It was not a duty for me.

My sister had moved on when she was young. She lived in England with her family. She had a job outside the home and had all the extras that I could never afford but did not need but of course she thought I did. Come over to me for a break she would say.

Break from what I would ask. I needed no break. I was happy where I was. In the evening when all the work was done I would walk down through the long meadow into the woods. There I would sit on the roots of the big old oak tree and thank god for all that I had. I knew what a lucky woman I was.

The kids started to repeat what my sister was saying. Go over to see how the rest of the world lives. Even my husband started it but I took no heed. Why do I need to go when I am happy where I am I constantly repeated.

Then one day they gave me a surprise for my birthday. They bought me a ticket to go to Manchester. My sister had taken the week off and was going to show me the sights of the city and then take me down to London.

I didn't really want to go but accepted the present with thanks. Maybe they were right. Maybe I did need to get away for a while. I knew in my heart that when I returned that I would appreciate even more what I had.

The kids were delighted the day they took me to the airport. They had never been to one before. Neither had I. I had never left the West. We had our tea there in the restaurant before we were parted. We never had been parted before. The kids had been born at home. There was no need to go anywhere.... We did go on holidays once to the coast of Clare. It was beautiful and we had a great time together. Just the four of us. My sister had come home and took care of Mammy and Daddy. I enjoyed it but back in my own kitchen, surrounded by my own things, I was once again reminded of how happy I was.

Mam and Dad hadn't come to the airport that day. I had said goodbye to them at the front door. Mam had handed me a ball of money in sterling. Get yourself something really nice she had said. Something that you always wanted but wouldn't spend the money on. I laughed. There is nothing I really want I replied. We had no television at the time so I had never seen all those lovely things that people think they need.

Mary met me at the airport, drove me through the city on the way to her home. How do you ever find your house I thought as she drove on and on and on? We had dinner and sat up chatting long after everyone else had retired. It must have been after two when we went to bed.

You sleep in as long as you want in the morning she said when she hugged me goodnight. It is long past your time to have a rest.

A few hours later the sound of something ringing woke me. What is that noise I thought for a moment and then I realized it was the sound of a telephone. Glad we don't have one of those I was thinking when Mary ran into the room and switched on the light. She was shaking. Tears were flowing down her face. She was unable to speak.

I jumped out of bed and took her into my arms.

'What's wrong I said? What's wrong Mary?'

She couldn't utter a sound. Her husband came in. I remember him slapping her on the face to bring her back. She was lost. She then started to scream until she was wasted. Then she whispered, 'they are all dead.'

'Who is dead I asked?'

'Mammy, Daddy, Tom, Mary and Johnny.'

'What do you mean dead?' I asked. I thought she had just lost her mind.

'I mean dead,' she replied. 'Dead. They were all burnt to death in a fire tonight. They were all burnt to death in their sleep…. They are all dead.'

I listened with horror to this story. Listened with disbelief. Could she possibly be making it up?

A few tears rolled down her face.

I asked,

'How did you make it home?'

She shook herself as if in a trance and replied,

'I have no idea. I know we all travelled together. That my neighbours picked me up at the airport. That they kept us all until after the funerals. They injected me in Manchester. Injected both me and Mary. Her husband had called the doctor. They did the same when I got home. I don't know what they gave me but it was for shock. I refused it after my whole family were buried. They told me I needed something to help me keep going. I told them I needed nothing. I grieved for two years. I thought I would die from grief….the shock, the numbness, the regret, the anger with myself for going away and with my sister for wanting me to go there. The depression, the pressure from friends and neighbours to blank it all with medication…. Then one day as I sat on the roots of the oak tree I realised that this was how it was meant to be. In that moment I was given the grace to understand and a renewed faith in God that has sustained me since.'

She continued: 'We are here to love ourselves and each other. We are here to love life. We are here to teach and to learn…. My family had all their teaching and learning and loving done. I will join them when I have finished mine.'

I sat opposite her and realised I was not in the company of an angel. I was in the company of a saint.

A Collection of Articles

Misdiagnosis

The Story of a "Cute" Schizophrenic

Written by Mary Lynch

The first time I met Margie was when she came to Foxford from Dublin with a group called Renew (www.renew-ireland.com). When I took them for a walk she was unable to come as she had not the energy; she was about fourteen stone in weight, bloated, and doped on prescription drugs. Her eyes were dead in her head, that same look I had seen in so many people that I had dispensed drugs to for years.

The second time I met her was outside a GAA centre in Offaly at a meeting of a network of people critical of the mental health model (CVN). I had gone outside for a breath of fresh air and talked to her as she stood there chain smoking.

When I asked her how she was her eyes and face lit up as she smiled and said, 'I'm going off all this shit they have me on.'

'Be careful,' I warned, 'your body can go into shock if the withdrawal process is not handled right.'

'I know,' she replied, 'I have done it cold turkey twice before and was so distressed that I tried to commit suicide. The last time I remember lying in a hospital bed listening to them tell my mother that there was no hope for me! There was so much damage done to my liver. It's a miracle that I am still alive. This time I know someone who will help me!'

The next time I met her was at a conference on mental health in UCC. We were staying in the same guesthouse. I had walked in for my breakfast and a woman in the corner had shouted over to me.

'Hi Mary, how are you?'

'Great,' I replied, 'and you?'

'Great,' she answered.

Who is she I was thinking as I continued to where my friend was sitting?

'Who is that woman who just spoke to me?' I asked him when I sat down.

He laughed and replied,

'I have no idea but she sure as hell knows you.'

Picking up the menu I held it at an angle so that I could peek over it and have another look. She caught my eye, waved and smiled.

When another lady arrived at our table I whispered, 'do you know that woman at the table at the window? Ah don't turn your head,' I pleaded as she turned to stare.

'Hi Margie,' she shouted over to her.

'Is that Margie?' I asked with shock.

'Yes,' she answered, 'did you not know her?'

'No,' I replied, 'what has she done with herself?'

'Lost over two stone in weight!' she replied.

I rose from the table and walked over to her and she said,

'You didn't know me Mary, did you?'

'No,' I replied honestly. 'How did you lose so much weight in the past six months, are you ok? What a stupid question,' I continued, 'you look great.'

'I started to go off my medication,' she said, 'and the weight just dropped off!'

'You're not doing it alone!' I exclaimed.

'No! with the help of the psychiatrist Dr. Ivor Browne,' she replied, 'and he is great.'

We didn't get a chance to talk anymore even though we travelled back to Dublin in the same car but as I was leaving her I said, 'Come down and stay with me in Foxford some time.'

'I will,' she replied.

Last week she arrived with another lady to help out her friend who was here in Ti Suaimhnis working her way through a stressful mental/emotional situation in a safe space where people understand what is happening.

She got out of the car and after giving her a hug I said without thinking,

'You look brilliant….. if I were to steal anyone's clothes I think I would steal yours.'

She was now four stone lighter and dressed with such style. 'How's the withdrawal process going?' I asked.

'Great,' she said, 'nearly off everything after eighteen years,' she added proudly.

Later when we went for a walk she said to me, 'was voted the most promising young designer in the early nineties…. less than a year later I was in a straight jacket in a psychiatric hospital!'

'What happened?' I asked shocked.

'I was on holiday in the Canaries with my friends. One night when we were out my drink was spiked and two men took me to a beach and raped me.'

'My God,' I said.

'I still don't remember everything, but afterwards I must have been walking around in a daze,' she continued, 'I eventually hailed down a taxi, I pulled all the money out of my pocket and asked him to take me to a resort on one of the other islands, one that I had been to with my family as a child. You know somewhere in my head I thought my mother would still be there and I would be safe. The taxi driver sensed something was seriously wrong but could speak very little English so he took me to his brother who somehow got my home number from me and called my mother. I was hysterical, she called my friends got the address and the taxi driver took me there. I went into my apartment and threw all my makeup and jewellery into the bin with all the clothes that I would never wear again as they were unsuitable as I thought it was because of them that this happened to me. I then started to put on all the rest of the clothes to cover my body. In all of this I was silent, like a zombie. I didn't trust any of my friends. I then ran to the beach and as everyone lay sunbathing I stripped off all the clothes and ran naked into the sea to drown myself. They got me out, got a towel around me and took me back to the apartment. The travel representative was called, she got a doctor and nurse and they injected me with another drug and put me into a straight jacket. I will never forget getting on that elevator screaming for someone to help me and when the elevator got to the ground floor the two men who had raped me were there in the lobby! The ambulance was like a Hiace van and I was so paranoid I didn't believe anyone of these people was trying to help me, I was sure it was a big conspiracy. I woke up later with my ankle chained to a bed. A man in a nurse's uniform that was dirty came in so I didn't believe he was for real and the room smelt of cigarette smoke. They tried in vain to get me to take medication which they called vitamins. I would take nothing but a doctor came in who had worked in Galway and he convinced me. From there I was taken out to a ward. A couple of days later as I was shuffling around in a pair of men's slippers that were a few sizes too big and borrowed pyjamas, drugged to the eyeballs I peeked into the doctor's office and saw my mother. I couldn't believe it was her, she was like an angel. She had flown out to take me home. Back in Dublin she took me to the local doctor and he sent me into John of Gods (psychiatric hospital).

I was labelled an acute schizophrenic, depressed, and then in 1995 I was told I was bipolar. Since then I have been on every anti-psychotic drug known to man, none of them worked as there was nothing wrong with me. That day I met you in Tullamore I also met Dr. Ivor Browne (the controversial retired psychiatrist and author) that had spoken out and said, 'When someone is depressed, [doctors] assume that this is caused by a disturbance in your biochemistry, which must be related to some sort of genetic thing in your personality. What I would want to know is what has happened in that person's past and their present that is disturbing their biochemistry and making them depressed?'

I asked him that day if he would help me get off the drugs. I was on 800mg of seroquel and sleeping tablets then. That was less than a year ago; I am now on 25mg and will be clean in the next few days.'

'Did you never tell any of the psychiatrists what happened to you?' I asked.

'I did,' she replied, 'and was told that you can imagine things when you are bipolar!'

She then smiled her big beautiful smile and said 'I now see a future now for myself Mary and will go back to designing; I haven't been able to hold down a job since the early nineties.'

They called her an acute schizophrenic - I think "cute" is a better word to describe her for she is now free of all the drugs that were forced on her! – One of the lucky ones.

Journey to Inner Light

I want to know what love is.

Written by Mary Lynch

'I was born out of a drunken rage' she told me. 'Had to be, to be hated so much by my parents'!
'I'm sure they did not hate you'. I answered.
'They hated me all right, resented me all their lives - I was never wanted'.
'Most of us were not planned in Catholic Ireland.' I replied. 'They had no choice!
'They had a choice to be cruel, or not. Mine choose to be cruel. Later in my life I would lie in bed and hear the abuse going on next door, and knew that is where I came from – abuse – not only a child that was abused, but, also a child that was born out of abuse'.
'What did your father work at?' I asked to lighten the subject.
'When he was not drinking...he was a labourer'.
'And what did he come from?'
'What do you mean?'
'Was he an abused child? - A child of alcoholic parents?' I asked
'Yes' she answered. 'Both my parents..... I remember the first night she sent me to the Gardai to get help, *for her*; I was a tiny child walking through the streets. Alone and frightened! She did not send my older brother. She sent me. She hated me. It was after twelve o clock at night, I had no choice but to go.

Woke out of my sleep. He then hated me more, for doing her bidding – I was the enemy – I was only a child. When a knock came to the door, they always told me to go pack my bags, that someone was coming to take me away. I still shake when I hear a knock – Still waiting for someone to take me away.

It was a neighbour on the street that was the first to abuse me - sexually', she continued, 'I was seven years old and I remember it as if it was yesterday. I did not know what was happening and had no one to tell – no one cared – still no one cares. What is it like to be loved Mary? I want to know what love is... After that it was as if I had a sign on me, abused child and my life was destroyed, it even started in the house then. I still lie awake at night, with the lights on and the radio playing. I cannot go to bed until it is nearly light, I am still afraid they will come back'.

'How do you keep going during the day?' I asked her when she stopped talking - This woman who's email I had replied to, when she wrote to me about my book, a woman so far removed from the border, that she had no idea what was going on in the north – the same age as me – suffering the same after-effects of trauma, but, stemming from a completely different source.

'I sleep at the weekends... during the day, and on my holidays'.

'Do you remember what happened to you?' I asked, remembering all the years that I had blanked.

'Yes, Everything! I have it all written down and hid in the house. No one knows what I have gone through'.

'Did you never think of going to counselling?'
'Yes. I go from time to time. It helps me survive, on a day to day basis, but, I will not tell her what happened to me in the past. Sometimes I sit there for an hour and say nothing - neither does she. I cannot stand silence, so, sometimes I just get up and leave... then I don't go back for weeks'.
'Why did you contact me?'
'I walked in to a bookshop, saw your book, and read it all that same night. I thought it was marvellous, knew you would understand, but, I did not expect a reply from you when I emailed. I have picked up the phone at least ten times in this past two weeks to call your number - could not finish it, sometimes I would go and get sick instead. I am sitting in the dark talking to you. I could not talk to you if the lights were on. I would not say what I am saying now'.
'Have you never told anyone this?'
'No, never! Who would listen, who would want to know? I am sorry I have kept you so long'.
'That is not a problem' I replied. 'I am glad you eventually called - Someday you will learn to trust'.
'No, I never could, I drank my way through college and was abused again'.
'What do you do when you are not working?' I asked
'I walk and walk and walk. Sometimes I drive and drive and drive'
'Why don't you drive and drive and come here, and we will walk and walk and talk and talk. There is a child in you and she needs to be loved' I urged.
'I know' she answered.

'She needs to be loved' I continued. 'And you are the one she needs the love from most, you will get so much more from others when you give it to yourself, you must look in the mirror and tell her that you love her'.

'I can't', she answered.

'You can', I replied. 'I know it's difficult at first, but it gets easier'.

'I can't,' she continued, 'I don't have a mirror in the house, I never look in a mirror, I cannot bear to look at myself, I hate myself, everyone else hates me too – I have no friends.

I go to work every day in sweatpants and tops, I don't want anyone to see any part of me. I even wear them in the summer'.

'What are you covering up', I asked. 'Apart from the abuse?

'Years of self abuse, I have razors all over the house and I cut myself when the pain of the memories are too much. It relieves me for awhile!'

She talked and talked, an hour later she said, 'I'd better let you go now'.

'It's ok,' I answered. 'Keep talking; say what you have to say'.

'How do you feel now?' I asked, when she had, eventually finished.

'Better' she replied. 'But, it will come back'.

'I know' I replied. 'Write it down and it will be out of your system'.

'I write all the time' she answered. 'But, it is still there'.

'Burn it and it will be gone...... I did!'

'But, then, no one will ever know what happened to me', she said... 'Would you read it, if I sent to you?'
I hesitated for a moment, and then replied.
'Yes, send it to me, I will read it, you will have given it to another human being and a burden shared is a burden halved'.
'Why would you do that for me? She asked.
'Because another human being did it for me. This is what love is – when one person reaches out to help another. You may not think you have a family but we are all the one family. I would not be here; strong enough to help you if I had not accepted help when it was offered. When you recover, and I know you can – You too can help another human being on the edge'.
'Thank you' she said. 'I will'.
She sent me a hand written account, by registered post, of all her abuse. To be honest I was a little afraid of it, afraid I would not have the strength to read it, but, next morning I reached for it as it lay on the locker at the side of my bed and together we burnt it as we shared a phone call that evening.
'I am so grateful to you' she said, 'but, I can't be bothering you anymore'.
'Come down to see me, to stay with me' I said. 'We will walk in the mountains'.
'I think I will' she said 'I can't believe you would do this for me'.
'We're friends'; I replied 'This is what friends do for each other'.
'I wouldn't know' she answered, 'I never had a friend before!'
I wished her a good night.

Next morning I had an email, thanking me, I returned it saying.
'Thank you too, I am blessed to have survived and honoured to be able to give something back, see you soon' Mary X

Personal Evolution : To become a butterfly?

Written by Karen Mc Dermott

I recently watched a David Attenborough wildlife program that showed the life cycle of a caterpillar. Not just an ordinary caterpillar this caterpillar lived in Siberia; a place where it was only sunny for a short period of the year and icy cold the rest.

The caterpillar would go around munching as much as it could all day long. It would munch, munch, munch. Then suddenly before it got to the cocoon stage the cold and ice came and the caterpillar froze. Amazingly when the sun came and the ice melted the caterpillar would come alive again and continue munching and munching and munching again in a desperate bid to eat a sufficient amount that it could reach the stage where it became a cocoon. But alas, this year was not to be its year either and the big frost came and the caterpillar froze again. Many cycles came and went and the caterpillar never lost faith that one day it would reach the stage at which it could find its sanctuary in the cocoon and so it continued to munch munch munch until finally the year came when before the ice came it turned into a cocoon and spared itself from another deep freezing. That year it became a butterfly which enabled it to fly to wherever it wanted to be.

It got me thinking and when I made a connection between the caterpillars quest and the quest that many of us humans pursue I was intrigued. I thought about how many of us keep munching and munching but give up before we reap the fruits of our labour. The caterpillar had faith, 100% belief, absolute unwavering knowing that it would make it, and against all of the odds it did. It may take many attempts but if we keep following our instinct then we will get there.

It is those people who are willing to work hard and persevere by weathering the storms they are rewarded especially when we follow our heart. That little caterpillar followed its heart, it so wanted to reach its goal and it instinctively knew how to get there, it is not as if it attended caterpillar school and was taught how to do it, no, it instinctively knew how to move forward, what it needed to do.

We will all get many opportunities to evolve during our lifetimes, we are ever changing beings. Some people choose to experience their life as only a caterpillar but for those who listen to their inner guide and move towards enlightenment by following their hearts desire, they will feel what it is like to live in the beauty and freedom that is being a beautiful butterfly.

Yes to become a butterfly you must work hard, however you will be guided through the process and before you emerge in all your glory you will have some time in your cocoon to rest, contemplate and prepare yourself for your new coming.

Journey to Inner Light

Are you a butterfly or are you content with being a caterpillar? Whatever path you choose remember that the butterfly knows what it is like to be a caterpillar but the caterpillar does not yet know what it is like to be a butterfly.

A COLLECTION OF ARTICLES

THE ANSWER IS LOVE

Written by Karen Mc Dermott

The answer to the question of all time is 'LOVE'.

What is the question? I hear you ask. The question is 'What is the key to true happiness?'

We all strive to be happy. No matter what circles we revolve in, our main goal is happiness. Whether it is materialistic or ambitious our end goal is achieving something that makes us, as individuals, feel happy.

Many people strive for perfection. But who is it that determines what perfection is? We all have our own ideals of perfection and aim for that and why? To make us HAPPY!

Now armed with this information that feeling love makes us happy. What are you going to do about it? How do you get enough love to make you happy? Well I am pleased to tell you that you don't need to go seeking; you just need to unlock the vault to your own self love. By loving ourselves we will discover true happiness that no amount of materialistic possessions will ever give us. When we access this love we will discover that there is a never-ending supply all for ourselves that we can share with others and it will never ever dry up. In fact the more we spread our love the more and more that is created and more and more that comes back to us.

I like to think of it as a snowball, by starting off with a little ball of love and giving it the opportunity to grow by rolling it along and nurturing it enabling it to become a greater ball of love. Then in no time at all it will be ready to roll down the mountain of life gathering more and more love all of the time. What do we have at the end? A great BIG ball of Love that everyone can feel and enjoy.

Did you know that we can heal our body and mind just by loving ourselves? Simply by taking the time to listen to the signals your body is giving you have the power within you to perform miraculous things.

"*Love creates miracles, Love creates magic*" Sascha Brooks

Louise L. Hay is a very inspiring woman and she passionately expresses how by loving yourself and affirming this love through positive affirmations you can heal ANY ailment or illness you may have. Yes, it is that amazing!

Tips on how to love yourself

Self-love may sound easy to do, but it is a process that needs focus and time to blossom. People who have suffered childhood neglect and abuse will find it very difficult to take the steps towards self love. Here are some tips I came across to assist in overcoming these steps.

Compile a list of things OTHERS like about you – ask people who know and love you what they like about you. This is a first step towards realising your personal qualities.

Write your own list of what YOU like about yourself – be honest to yourself, if you are having trouble think about the people you love and the qualities you admire in them. Do you have those same qualities?

Feel good notebook/box: Invest in a notebook or box that makes you feel good when you see it. Use it to keep these lists in. Look at its contents every time that you feel low or if you are made feel low by someone else.

Read as much as possible – Make reading these wonderful things about you a regular occurrence in your life, as many times as you can. Every time you do, it will eliminate one time you felt bad or were made feel bad and replace it with a positive.

Add a note- Make yourself tune in to hearing the positives about you no longer the negatives. Write each of them down and add them to your collection.

You are your own best friend – We all love our friends but I have news for you, YOU are your own best friend, love yourself as do your friends. Close your eyes, feel the love you have for them and project it onto yourself. Store that feeling.

Give yourself a break – Learn to be compassionate and forgiving to yourself. Would you be so hard and judgemental on your friends or loved ones? No you would probably be there offering support. Fell that love and compassion for your-self.

Love comes within – A well of love exists within us all we can access it whenever we choose. Access self love regularly. You deserve to be loved so love yourself.

Affirmations – By using affirmations you are registering positives in your brain which will help you to feel good. Things like: I am an amazing loving and caring person. I deserve the very best in my life. I am a loving and caring person. Pin them up in the areas you are in most often car, computer, fridge, work. Feel them.

Nurture yourself – Do things for yourself that make you feel loved and cared for. A nice pampering session, some meditation, a wonderful book that we enjoy, a peaceful walk. These are some things that we can gift to ourselves which will enhance our loving potential.

Listen - Take a quiet moment to listen to yourself and the signs that you are receiving. It may take time to connect but by giving yourself some time each day to listen to your inner guide you will recognise your needs and desires easier.

Look – This will be a hard one for many. I know for me it was. Look in a mirror, look straight into your eyes and tell yourself "I love you" do this every day as much as you feel comfortable with and you will find that it will get easier. I found it very emotional the first time I did it. For me the eyes are the gateway to the soul and I felt an intense feeling at that moment.

These are all tips that you can use to assist on your journey to self-love. You need only select the ones that you feel will work for you. It can be hard to give yourself this gift at first but always know that you have the courage and strength within you and you deserve it!

The love that you attract from others comes from you initially. If you don't love yourself then it is really hard for others to love you. I know this because I went through a period where I did not take the time to love me. I was just motoring along, loving my family and doing what I thought was right. But it wasn't o.k. my relationships were straining around me and I was not being fulfilled, my soul was perishing. Since learning to love myself I radiate love and in every aspect of my life all of my relationships have blossomed too. I have so much love now within and I know that I will always glow.

When I talk about loving myself I don't mean being arrogant; this is when someone thinks only of them self. No, Self-love is when someone has a strong sense of respect for and confidence in themselves. This is usually taught in childhood through honesty, acceptance and unconditional love. However most parents have their own issues of self-doubt and limiting beliefs which they project onto their children consciously and un-consciously and so a cycle of self-rejection repeats itself.

So let's break the cycle and stigma attached to self-love. In order to truly love another we need to love ourselves first. It is important not only for us but for our families and for humanity. Everything in life will be better now that we know 'The Answer'

"Love is the great miracle cure. Loving ourselves works miracles in our lives." Louise L Hay

A Collection of Articles

SPIRITUALITY

Written by Karen Mc Dermott

"The meaning of spirituality is diving deep into inner self and realizing our true identity. The spirit within! It is only through path of spirituality that human beings have gained enlightenment."

I think that being or becoming Spiritual is to progress within ourselves, to be able to love ourselves and others unconditionally and also to have the ability to forgive more easily. It is a personal process which we may or may not choose to embark on in our lifetime, but it is widely recognised that those who do embark on their spiritual journey arrive at a point of personal fulfilment like none other. Connecting with our soul and helping it flourish to its highest potential; the most beautiful experience of all for many.

When talking about Spirituality I am not talking about going to a regular service because you think it is the right thing to do or because you feel that you have to. I mean going within and then going to a service from that point if that is what you feel meets with your personal spiritual requirements and beliefs.

In this era that we reside there is so much horror and devastation on global levels and personal levels for many. Belief in the fact that there is a higher source with our best intensions its main focus, ensuring that we are protected and that our needs and desires are being taken care of, is quite a comforting thought; especially through times of uncertainty.

If every human being recognised the power of the love and forgiveness principle, all consciousness on Earth would change instantly" Kuan Yin.

Forgiveness

The ability to forgive ourselves and others is a gift. This gift must not be abused or taken advantage of. This ability allows us to learn and move on in progression through our journey of life. When I speak of forgiveness for ourselves I don't mean someone who does not want to learn from their wrong-doing, these people are just being wreck less but maybe at some point on their journey through life they may awaken to experience the beauty of getting to look at the world from within.

Giving.

The ability to give to others is not only a gift to them but a gift to ourselves because we are also giving ourselves the wonderful feeling of giving. And by doing so we are creating more opportunities for others to give and experience the same feeling themselves. In order to have the honour that giving is we must be open to receiving also. This cycle is a soul enhancing experience. By using the word giving I am expressing giving our time, energy and love; however for some the giving of a material gift is used to represent their affections. "It is the thought that counts".

5 Stages of the soul

It is usually when we start to query our being that we ask ourselves questions. I am reading a book called 'The 5 stages of the Soul' by Harry R Moody and David Carroll. It expresses how each of transcend through different stages when we connect within. "Is this all there is?" is often a trigger question which instigates an urge to explore our spirituality as fulfilment in material and ambitious driven targets do not feed the soul.

1. **The Call**: First step in the pursuit of spiritual wisdom. In history some have recorded dramatic callings, like the roar from an ocean or other physical callings, but for most of us the CALL comes in less dramatic ways. Like something just clicks or something occurs that draws us internally to start our journey. This can happen at any age or stage of our life cycle.
2. **The Search**: Our response to 'The Call' is with a 'Search'. This happens for most by a search for guidance. A search for a spiritual teaching path or a seeking after a place within us where our spiritual impulse lives and grows. "We must try to rediscover the Friend in our hearts every moment. Our search is to keep remembering what we already know"
3. **The Struggle**: Our guidance is discovered and our soul's true passage begins. This occurs in a cosmic dimension as well as a human one. Enduring

challenges, trials or passing tests all may present themselves during this stage. These challenges can range from depression to debt to work issues to relationship issues to name a few. To reach the goal we must face the challenges head on.

4. **The Breakthrough**: And then there was peace! Just like a miracle we will catapult to a state of at-oneness with something beyond ourselves. A sudden surge of energy pushes things to the limit; then follows a burst of vision and the hidden forces of the world force to our consciousness. Something has changed in us, and we are never the same. Now known by some as 'The Changed Ones'.

5. **The Return**: Life still goes on as before, but we now have a knowledgeable insight and understanding to give back to the world. Some may be a better more giving individual others may become deeply committed to services or humanitarian projects. For those who experience a deeper experience of 'The Breakthrough' will likely develop a guide or mentor.

Spiritual Practices

Meditation, Prayer and Contemplation are all used as techniques to develop our inner growth. It is believed that these practices lead to experiencing a feeling of connectedness to a larger reality. This can lead to a deeper sense of fulfilment within us and with others, nature and the universe. This can enable a person to discover the essence of their being; or the "deepest values and meanings by which people live."

Others may look outside of themselves to project blame onto a higher source. I would like to challenge that and ask that we go within and take on board our little piece of responsibility of how the world is changing. Maybe if we all were that little more loving and little more forgiving there would not be so much uncertainty.

For me Spirituality is getting to the point within myself where I can love unconditionally MYSELF and Others. No matter what happens the ability to forgive and project love to even those who do us wrong is true divine peace within oneself.

I expect that as I progress on my eternal path to enlightenment that my knowledge on Spirituality will also progress. This is however how I have come to understand a concept that is often thought of as complex but if you take the time to listen to your inner guide you will soon discover that it is all quite simple.

"The gifts we can receive from people who have tasted spiritual possibility are maps which we then use to guide our own journey." Ram Dass

Christie Lyons

A COLLECTION OF ARTICLES

STARTING TO HEAL

Written by Christie Lyons

Just a few weeks before Christmas, I lost my baby. The most common term used is miscarriage, or as the hospital called it when they released me from the emergency department, 'spontaneous abortion'. I prefer to refer to it as a baby, because it gives much more meaning to the fact that I lost a living being that was beginning to grow inside of me. It just seems too cold and clinical to call it any of those other medical terms, and considering that carrying a child is such a beautiful and miraculous event, I think it at least deserves the acknowledgement of a more significant term.

After two agonising weeks of constant tests and hospital visits, my husband and I were finally told the news that we were dreading to hear, and I felt like my heart was being ripped out of my chest as the doctor uttered the words. I felt physical pain from the heartbreak I was experiencing and although it was only early on in the pregnancy, it hurt all the same. Our baby was already gone.

Being just eight weeks pregnant when I lost my baby, I honestly struggled at first to allow myself to grieve. I had this inane belief that I wasn't allowed to be so upset because it was so early on in my pregnancy, and being such a common occurrence, I should somehow 'suck it up' and move on because it happened so often. Although I had such a strong support network of friends and family around me, it wasn't until my they were adamant that I stay at home and grieve that I began to allow myself to rightfully be upset about my loss.

During this time at home, I started to research. I needed to know more about why this had happened and looked everywhere I could for answers. I came across several different theories about miscarriage and the reasoning behind it, but the medical answers weren't enough for me. I needed a deeper meaning for my loss. It was during this search for meaning that I came across Karen McDermott's book 'The Visitor'. Her story helped me to grieve, and it allowed me to give the loss of my baby more significance.

As I read Karen's words, I began to feel a connection with her and so I joined the Adopt a Mum network, where I was able to find support from not only Karen, but a wonderful group of like-minded souls. Although these were people that I had never met, I felt such a sense of comfort among this group and it was thanks to them that my passion for writing was reignited. Karen invited me to contribute my story to her new book that was being published and I felt so honoured that I started working on it straight away.

Through writing, I was able to record all the emotions I had felt throughout the events of my life, and by the time I had reached the loss of my baby, I realised that I was beginning to heal. Writing about my journey was a wonderfully therapeutic process and I was finally able to truly let go of some of my past hurts and negative emotions. I genuinely felt like a brand new person after completing my story. I felt rejuvenated, my hope was renewed, and I was excited about my future. My desire to write had been restored and I began to explore another passion of mine that had gone awry, my spirituality.

The months that have passed since losing this beautiful soul have been nothing short of extraordinary. For the first time in a long time, I feel a newfound confidence and I am genuinely happy. I have been able to focus on my creative interests and have made sure I take time out to do so. My relationships with my husband and family have improved immensely, and every aspect of my life seems to be falling into perfect synchronicity. I have been writing to my heart's content, reading and researching all the many wondrous aspects of the spiritual world, and all the while, everything around me seems to be harmonious.

Although losing my baby was one of the saddest times of my life, I also believe that it happened for a reason. If I hadn't experienced it, I don't believe that I would have explored my past wounds in so much depth, which means that I might not have truly been given the opportunity to heal. I will be forever grateful to my little angel for giving me the chance to start again.

I WAS THERE ALL ALONG!

Written by Christie Lyons

The past few months have been such a turning point in my life, and I now truly understand what people mean when they say they have 'found themselves'. In the last six months or so, my life has changed, and I feel a sense of peace and fulfilment right now that has seemingly appeared from nowhere.

Who would have thought that through the loss of my baby late last year, that something so wonderful could happen to me so soon? Now, some people may be thinking to themselves "Wow, what's happened? It must be something big!" Well, something big has happened, but it might not quite be what you think.

Since this awful moment in my life, not only have I found my love for writing again, but it also pushed me further forward in finding out more about myself spiritually. This event forced me to take time out for myself, where I started to read and research as much as I could, and I have even learnt to love myself again. I'm finding myself being more and more thankful for the people and the things I do have, but importantly for me, I have learnt to say 'no' and have a newfound confidence to stand up for what I believe in.

My life is all starting to make sense, and I often have to pinch myself because I am feeling so happy and at peace. My true passions are coming to the surface, and for the first time in a very long time, I have interests other than work. For many years, I spent all my spare moments engulfed in work, and it was my only hobby. While I still adore my career in early childhood, I am now pursuing other passions in my spare time. The most fascinating thing about this is that I am actually allowing myself to *have* spare time.

Over many, many years, I hid beneath all the trauma, challenges and dramas that I have experienced throughout my life, and never really worked through them. It wasn't until I started writing about them and letting them out that I was able to really allow myself to *feel* the feelings that I should have felt at the time. Once I had been through that process, it allowed me to release all the negativity behind these events, and simply learn from them and be grateful for the wisdom and strength those experiences had given me.

While it took a tragic moment for all of this to happen, I am so very blessed to have been given the opportunity to find my true self once again. I was lost for quite a while, but I now realise that I was there all along; I just needed to be patient until I was ready to *be* again.

My Jellybean

Written by Christie Lyons

I have never in my life been so happy to be feeling sick. I have no energy, I want to sleep all the time, and it feels as though I have a constant hangover, but it gives me so much comfort in knowing that the beautiful life growing inside of me is healthy and happy.

I am only in my eighth week of pregnancy, but I know that everything is going to be perfectly okay. When hubby and I went for our first scan a couple of days ago, I must admit I was nervous, as the last time we had been for this type of scan, we were told that we had lost our baby. As soon as we were shown our little bub on the screen and were told there was a good, strong heartbeat, I breathed a sigh of relief, knowing that this little one was here to stay.

It still amazes me just how much my life has changed in the last six months, and I continue to believe that this little jellybean was waiting to come to us for a reason. All these wonderfully positive changes needed to occur beforehand; not only with me, but for my husband as well. Our last little angel gave us both the push we needed to find ourselves once again, and for our little family to be harmonious before we received another addition. I will be forever thankful to our little angel baby for giving us this beautiful gift.

I know that our family is ready to have this beautiful baby join us, and that my son is so ready to be a big brother. Brendon is such a kind, caring soul, and I can't wait to see the look on his face when he meets his baby brother or sister. This little one will certainly be very lucky to have him as their big brother and he will be someone that will protect, guide and support them from the moment they come into this world.

While I still grieve for our angel baby we lost a few months ago, I do have faith in the fact that this was all meant to happen the way that it did. I will never forget the little one that we lost, but I do know that they will be watching over us all as their little brother or sister comes into this world; knowing that we are now ready to have this child join our happy little family.

About Inner Light Publishing

Inner Light Publishing was founded in 2012 with the intention of sharing inspiring stories with the world.

We are proud to present this collection of stories that, we hope, may have a positive influence on someone's life.

We want to assist authors of all genres get published in a positive way and so we have put together a collection of publishing packages to help aspiring authors.

If you would like to share your inspiring story for our next collection you can contact us at innerlightpublishing@gmail.com

Inner Light Publishing would not be if it were not for our affiliation with adoptamum.com.

Building Beautiful Bonds

Your inspiring journey

Use this space to jot down your story and thoughts

www.ingramcontent.com/pod-product-compliance
Lightning Source LLC
Chambersburg PA
CBHW031243290426
44109CB00012B/418